A HEARTY BAND OF FIREFIGHTERS

In this 1970s photo a pair of firefighters wet down a fire. In a particularly hot and close fire the lead pipe man would sometimes reverse his helmet as a heat and debris shield.

THE
DONNING COMPANY
PUBLISHERS

A HEARTY BAND OF FIREFIGHTERS

The Illustrated History of the Danvers Fire Department

By
Chief Leland E. Martin, Jr.
Edited by
Richard P. Zollo
With an Introduction by
Richard B. Trask

**1997
A PUBLICATION OF THE
DANVERS HISTORICAL SOCIETY
DANVERS, MASSACHUSETTS**

This book is dedicated
to the loyal members of the
Danvers Fire Department,
past and present.

Copyright © 1997 by Danvers Historical Society

All rights reserved, including the right to reproduce this work in any form whatsoever without permission in writing from the publishers, except for brief passages in connection with a review. For information, write:

The Donning Company/Publishers
184 Business Park Drive, Suite 106
Virginia Beach, VA 23462

Steve Mull, General Manager
Debra Y. Quesnel, Project Director
Tracey Emmons-Schneider, Director of Research
Sally C. Davis, Editor
Betsy Bobbitt, Graphic Designer
Dawn V. Kofroth, Assistant General Manager
Teri S. Arnold, Senior Marketing Coordinator

Library of Congress Cataloging-in-Publication Data

Martin, Leland E., 1926–
 A hearty band of firefighters: the illustrated history of the Danvers Fire Department/by Leland E. Martin, Jr.; edited by Richard P. Zollo; with an introduction by Richard B. Trask.
  p.   cm.
 "A publication of the Danvers Historical Society."
 Includes bibliographical references and index.
 ISBN 1–57864–011–3 (softcover: alk. paper)
 1. Danvers (Mass.). Fire Dept.—History. 2. Fire extinction—Massachusetts—Danvers—History. 3. Fires—Massachusetts—Danvers—History. 4. Fire fighters—Massachusetts—Danvers. I. Zollo, Richard P., 1926–   . II. Danvers Historical Society. III. Title.
TH9505.D2504M38   1997
363.37'09744'5—dc21   97-29889
                                           CIP

Printed in the United States of America

CONTENTS

FOREWORD	*By Deputy Chief Richard C. Wessell*	6
PREFACE		11
ACKNOWLEDGMENTS		13
INTRODUCTION	Looking Back: The Early History of Firefighting in Danvers *By Richard B. Trask*	15
CHAPTER ONE	Reorganization Under Chief Kelley	45
CHAPTER TWO	Wartime Activities	55
CHAPTER THREE	The 1850 Maple Street Church Leveled	61
CHAPTER FOUR	Adventures of a Young Danvers Firefighter	69
CHAPTER FIVE	Firemen's Musters and Forest Fires	81
CHAPTER SIX	Arson at Putnam Lodge; Death of James Horgan	83
CHAPTER SEVEN	School Street Inferno; The End of Parker's Gristmill	95
CHAPTER EIGHT	Chelsea and Lynn Burn; Nesson Block Gutted	105
CHAPTER NINE	Local Heroes Cited for Bravery	113
CHAPTER TEN	Beaver Park Catastrophe	123
CHAPTER ELEVEN	Oil Rig and Boat Fires	141
AFTERWORD		149
APPENDIX ONE	A list of the major firefighting apparatus acquired by the Danvers Fire Department, 1800–1997	154
APPENDIX TWO	Firemen 1900–1910	164
APPENDIX THREE	Firefighters of the 20th Century	166
APPENDIX FOUR	Duty Roster for 1997 Danvers Fire Department	170
INDEX		172

FOREWORD

Leland E. Martin, Jr.'s first interest in the fire service occurred on May 12, 1935, when Box 15 was transmitted at 6:15 a.m. for a fire at Batchelder's Ice House at the Mill Pond. At the time, Marty was nine years old and lived with his parents on Chase Street. He was fortunate to have as a neighbor and mentor, Joseph E. Kelley, Sr., who was Fire Chief in Danvers from 1925–1958. On this day, Marty's mother, Mrs. Kelley, and Marty walked from Chase Street to the Mill Pond where they watched the ice house being destroyed by fire. Ironically, on November 13, 1960, at 5:45 p.m., Marty returned to the Batchelder property. This time it was for a major barn fire which was located across the street from where the ice house fire had occurred. The barn was located to the rear of the Putnam homestead at 33 Holten Street. This property is now the Holten Garden Condominiums. From boyhood on, Marty was "hooked" on the profession of firefighting.

His neighbor and mentor, Fire Chief Joseph E. Kelley, Sr., encouraged him to visit the fire stations and to participate in the various functions and activities of the department, including the fighting of fires (at this time, liability was a term that was unheard of). When the audible fire whistle sounded an alarm of fire, he would run or ride his bike down Bayview Avenue to High Street where he would meet either Engine 3 going toward Danvers Square or Engine 1 or Ladder 5 heading for Danversport. One of these companies would stop and pick him up and off they would go to the fire. What a great thrill for a young man to experience at this age!

Marty was an individual who took great pride not only in his community, but in his country. While still in his junior year at high school, Marty felt a very strong sense of calling to join the war effort. On July 22, 1944, he walked down Bayview Avenue, boarded the bus for Boston, and enlisted in the United States Navy at the Fargo Building. He was assigned as a coxswain aboard the U.S.S. *Chicago* stationed in the South Pacific. He was present at the signing of the armistice in Tokyo Harbor when the Japanese surrendered at the end of World War II. On May 22, 1946, Marty was discharged from the U.S. Navy.

On June 29, 1947, he was appointed to the department. I can recall Marty telling me the story that on his first day as a paid firefighter he had dropped his car off to be repaired in Danvers Square. He then walked up Maple Street, paused in front of Headquarters, looked up at the front of the building which would be his home away from home for the next forty-five years and said to himself, "Someday I'm going to be Chief."

From day one, Marty was never an individual to run away from adversity or a difficult situation. He was always the first one into a burning building and the last one out.

Marty had a tremendous thirst for education and a very strong desire to improve on his abilities as a firefighter. Shortly after he joined the department, it was determined that all future captains would come under the Civil Service process. When Marty learned of this, he started to study for the exam which was eventually held in 1951. He spent most of his free time studying. The more knowledge he obtained, the greater his thirst became. When he took the exam he obtained a grade of 90.42. While not the top mark, it was good enough to put him in contention for one of the captain's positions. At the time he had very little practical experience and was the youngest man on the department. He was passed over for the position, a situation that was devastating at the time, but which he stated to me on many occasions, was the best thing that ever happened to him and his career.

Not to be discouraged, he picked himself up by his boot straps and made a promise to himself that the next captain's job would be his. He became friends with John Clougherty, who at the time was a captain with the Boston Fire Department and later went on to become Chief of the Department. Captain Clougherty ran classes for promotion in his home in Charlestown on a weekly basis for those students who would meet his standards and commit themselves to the rigorous study schedule he required to keep pace with the rest of the class. In 1958 Marty took the Civil Service exam for captain and passed with a grade of 93.07. On November 13, 1958, he was appointed captain on the Danvers Fire Department. At this time the department had three captains in charge of three groups; Captain Rollie Sturtevant, Captain Joe Kelley, Jr., and Captain Phil Davis. Marty was assigned as the junior captain working under Captain Joe Kelley, Jr. In this position, he rode the ladder truck and filled in for vacations and sickness on all three groups.

I first met Marty in 1958. At that time I was running my own landscape contracting business, and employing off-duty firefighters on a part-time basis. This made it necessary to visit the fire station several times a week. As time went by, I became more and more interested in firefighting and developed friendships with several members of the department. I was living in the Town of Boxford at this time. Through the encouragement of members of the Danvers Fire Department, I joined the call department in Boxford whose fire department was in desperate need of professional training. Having become friendly with Marty and being aware of his dedication to education and training, I asked if he could help us establish a training program for the Town of Boxford. Not only did he set up a program, but he personally came to Boxford one night a week for a prolonged period of time and ran the program. It was at this time that I realized the strong commitment that this man had, not only to the Town of Danvers but toward the fire service as a whole.

On December 3, 1960, Marty once again distinguished himself as one who put the safety and well-being of others ahead of his own. At 2:00 a.m. several telephone calls were received for a house fire at 30 North Belgian Road. Upon our arrival, the owners, Mr. and Mrs. Blosofsky, were found on the front lawn in a dazed condition. They had just leapt through a bedroom window after a vain attempt to locate their daughter had failed. They directed Marty to Laura's bedroom window. Marty cleaned out the window, entered the structure and found the child unconscious on the bedroom floor. He removed her from the room to the outside where after several minutes, she was revived and transported to the Hunt Hospital.

During his early years as a firefighter, Marty had worked as a carpenter part-time for Max Berry, who was a building contractor in the Town of Danvers. The skills which Marty learned while working for Mr. Berry as a carpenter, served not only to hone his skills as a firefighter, but also taught him the finer points of building construction. In addition, it provided him with the knowledge and ability to build two homes with his own hands (18 Shetland Road and 9 Greenleaf Drive) which he and his family resided in over the years. This love for woodworking resulted in a hobby which he enjoyed the rest of his life. In addition to his woodworking skills, he had a great love for gardening and photography. He did both with a very caring and professional touch. Anyone visiting Marty was always given a tour of his backyard gardens.

As I indicated, Marty was a very strong believer of education. He devoted a portion of each day to reading and studying fire related material. Around 1963, Marty and Joe O'Keefe (originator of the Fire Science Program at North Shore Community College and former State Fire Marshal) established a course in fire department administration for interested members of the Danvers Fire Department. This course was held at Danvers Fire Headquarters and was the forerunner of the fire science program at North Shore Community College. In 1967, Marty enrolled in the first Fire Science Program to be offered in the area at North Shore Community College. He graduated on June 12, 1974, with a degree in Fire Science with honors.

On May 5, 1982, Marty was appointed by Governor Edward King as a member of the Board of Trustees of North Shore Community College. This had a very special meaning to Marty as he credited N. S. C. C. with providing him with the educational opportunity and skills necessary to become an administrator and Chief of the Department during the 1970s and 1980s. In 1991, North Shore Community College presented Marty with its Distinguished Alumni Award. On June 4, 1992, Governor William Weld reappointed Marty as a member of the Board of Trustees of N. S. C. C. for a term which would have expired on March 1, 1997.

Over the years, Marty formed a bond with a group of fire chiefs that developed into a friendship, trust, and camaraderie which is seldom seen today. The members of the elite group, which was called the "Billy-B-Damns," included Dean Palmer (Beverly), Jim Brennan (Salem), Skip Emerson (Ipswich), John Quinn (Nahant), Ed Creighton (Marblehead), and Marty. This was a group of outstanding individuals that bonded together in friendship with the intent of sharing their ideas, having a good time, and striving to improve the fire service as a whole. The attitude was always all for one and one for all. Even to this day, the remaining members of the group always include the wives of the deceased members in their plans and activities.

Marty was a man of compassion and friendship. I can recall him loaning money to several individuals with no provisions for pay back or interest required. I can recall the day when he purchased a bike for a young man because his family could not afford it. I have been with him on more than one occasion at ten or twelve o'clock at night in someone's kitchen trying to help a man solve a problem. I have also witnessed him provide everything from food and lodging, his own time and expertise, books, and counseling, etc. to those in need.

On July 21, 1991, after forty-five years, one month and one day of service to the Town of Danvers Fire Department, Marty retired. He was a person who strived for excellence, always did the job to the best of his ability, was quick to admit when he was wrong, and never held a grudge. It wasn't always easy wearing the gold badge during this era, nor is it easy today. Collective bargaining has a tendency to create a wall or barrier between the rank and file and the front office. Other than times of negotiations, Marty had a good rapport with the rank and file and they respected his abilities and expertise as a firefighter.

I can recall very vividly Marty's last day on the job. The usual jokes, the kidding, and the smiles were not there. I could sense the feeling of sadness as he cleaned out his personal belongings from his desk. I observed his facial expressions as he paused to read a clipping about the past or looked at a photograph which brought back fond memories of days gone by. I would take over his job as Acting Chief on that day until such time as a permanent chief could be named. I recall very clearly the advice he imparted to me. He said, "You will have many rewarding days, and there will be some days that you will go home and wonder if you could have done better, and also if you had done this instead of what you did do, the ultimate end would have been different. Just do the best you can, and if you do fail try, try again." This pretty much expressed his own philosophy on the way he felt as he experienced his tenure as chief. As the hour of 5:00 p.m. neared, you could sense the stress in the room and feel the sadness in the air. I asked him if he would like me to give him a ride home. He declined. We embraced each other; we were both choked up and had a difficult time speaking as he left his office for the last time as Chief of Department. As I was sitting in my living room that night about 9:00 p.m., I head over the fire radio Marty's last message as Chief of Department. "This is C-1 signing off the air for the last time." He had parked his car at the rear of the station and walked home to 9 Greenleaf Drive. I would imagine that this was probably the longest and loneliest walk of his entire life.

On Friday, September 13, 1991, a retirement party was held at the Danversport Yacht Club. The Master of Ceremonies was Ed Creighton, former Chief of the Marblehead Fire Department. Approximately three hundred people were in attendance, people from all walks of life, people who had touched his life in many ways. Among the well wishers that evening, who had traveled a considerable distance to give Marty a proper send-off, were four former Pease Air Force firefighters who turned the Danvers Fire House into a home away from home some twenty-five years ago. All four were sparkies that were welcomed and encouraged by Marty.

Frank Gorup was with the U.S. Department of Energy in Naperville, IL.; Don Ford was an Assistant City Manager in Pontiac, IL.; Jim Erickson had become a Deputy Fire Chief in Hartford, CT.; and Jack Fray was an insurance executive in Madison, VA. This group turned the retirement party into a reunion as well which touched Marty deeply. As Frank Gorup said, "Marty and Danvers took in four lonely servicemen and taught them how to fight fires from 1962–1966."

On Sunday, October 30, 1994, at the age of sixty-eight, Marty passed away. His funeral was held on Wednesday, November 2, 1994, at the Maple Street

Congregational Church with full fire department honors. Interment was at the Wadsworth Cemetery on Summer Street.

I lost a good friend and mentor that day, a man who had taught me a lot, encouraged me along the way and stood beside me when I needed a friend. I will always remember him and be thankful for the legacy he left behind. As Marty used to say whenever he left someone, "God Bless." I think this poem which was found with Marty's memorabilia best describes Marty.

"How Do You Measure Success"
Author Unknown

To laugh often and much
To win the respect of intelligent people,
and the affection of children
To earn the appreciation of honest critics
and to endure the betrayal of false friends
To appreciate beauty—to find the best in others
To leave the world a bit better
whether by a healthy child,
A garden patch. A redeemed social condition
or a job well done.
To know even one other life has breathed easier
Because you have lived
This is to have succeeded....

This was how Marty lived and worked.

RICHARD C. WESSELL
Deputy Fire Chief

Deputy Fire Chief Richard C. Wessell directing firefighting activities at an April 7, 1996, fire at 24 Maple Street in Danvers Square. Deputy Wessell retired from the department in July 1997.

PREFACE

Throughout his long career on the Danvers Fire Department, Chief Leland E. Martin, Jr. regarded firefighting as an exciting adventure full of danger and heroism. His account of those years in *A Hearty Band of Firefighters* is replete with a never flagging zest for his life's work. What he wrote is a combination of historical data and personal narrative. While Chief Martin fought hundreds of fires, he carefully selected many of his most challenging ones to describe to his readers.

As a result, Marty's narrative gains in interest as he takes up more and more serious conflagrations, climaxing in the 1990 Beaver Park catastrophe during which he proved himself up to the task. Standing at Point Zero, he is totally in charge of the complex events swirling around him. He is a general on the field of combat commanding forces from twenty-seven different communities with forty-five fire companies and one hundred and forty-seven firefighters. The Chief brings a vividness to the fireground few of his peers have equalled.

In 1990–1991, Marty approached several of us in the Danvers Historical Society for assistance in putting his manuscript into publishable form. Toni Collins, Ann McNamara, Richard Trask, and I gave him some help on format and a few mechanics of expression. Ann correctly described his work (he called it a paper) as "worthwhile material." We all recognized its merits, but funding for a published volume was not available at that time. Whenever publication did become possible, Richard Trask and I pledged that we would provide for Leland Martin's history the type of volume we had produced with Curator Joan Reedy in 1989—*As the Century Turned: Photographic Glimpses of Danvers, 1880–1910.*

In 1991, Chief Martin ran off in very limited numbers his manuscript under the title *A History of the Danvers Fire Department.* These he gave to his friends and fellow firefighters. A few copies of it are on file at the Danvers Archival Center. While I have always remained anonymous as an editor, it is necessary to point out here steps that were taken to organize his material for an illustrated history.

For a general readership, I have arranged his original text into chapters and broken long paragraphs into shorter ones. As far as the chapters are concerned, in a few instances it was necessary to provide a sentence or two of transition. Chapter One has the longest bridge because it serves the dual function of introduction and segue from Dick Trask's history of the nineteenth-century fire companies to Chief Martin's of the Danvers Fire Department in the twentieth. While Marty had several pages on the previous century, it was felt that a fuller account of that era would provide a more comprehensive history.

Because Marty's first audience was, for the most part, fellow firefighters, he didn't often provide explanations for technical terms like gate, charge or advance a line, triple combination engine, supply or feeder lines, overhauling, etc. Identification was not needed for his readership, but it is for a broader one. More information has been given on the manufacturers of fire apparatus for the same reason. Richard Trask served as photo editor for the project, choosing illustrations and writing captions to go along with them.

A minor omission a few readers may notice in the text is that of fire commissioners, the one-time civilian heads of the fire department. However, by the time Marty became chief, the town had long dispensed with their services, an action that took place after the change to the manager form of government in 1949.

I'm aware of their absence because my father, Paul G. Zollo, was one of the two commissioners who served together from 1945–1949. An old spark, he was conscientious about his work. I can recall him spending hours preparing for finance committee and town meetings to justify the expense of new equipment. It was during the post–war period when, according to Marty, the Danvers Fire Department was becoming "second to none" in Essex County.

An advocate of better trained and educated firefighters and an instructor of the latest firefighting techniques at North Shore Community College, this Chief would have found the presence of untrained non-professionals like the commissioners in the department inappropriate. As far as the men of the Danvers Fire Department were concerned, Marty loved their close comradeship and traditions so much that he wrote his history to preserve their spirit and their brave actions.

Among the volumes I utilized as editor were two on fire engines by Sheila Buff and T. A. Jacobs and two training texts for firefighters: *Essentials of Firefighting* and Warren Kimball's *Fire Department Terminology*. Quoted in the section on the School Street inferno was a *Salem Evening News* article, "Blaze Rips Danvers Warehouses," by Bill Cahill, printed on January 9, 1967.

R. P. Z.

ACKNOWLEDGMENTS

Many people have assisted in putting together this volume, including defining terminology, checking facts, and loaning photographs. This book is also indebted to present and past photographers whose work is reproduced here including: Thomas J. O'Connor; Roger L. Cyr; Joseph F. Briggs; Willard Allphin; M. H. Keohane; the *Danvers Herald* and Bill Woolley and David Spink (including the photographs reproduced in Chapter Ten); the *Salem Evening News*; Kirk R. Williamson; Richard L. Oulton; Ed Wolkin; Eddie Richers; C. W. Avery; and Francis J. Carbone.

Grateful acknowledgment is noted to the following people and institutions: Deputy Chief Richard C. Wessell; Mrs. Leland E. Martin, Jr.; Robert G. Osgood; Ann McNamara; Betty Jones; Edward McLaughlin; Marjorie Wetzel; Myrna Fearer; Howard Iverson; Wilfred (Fred) Vaillancourt; Toni Collins; Barbara Harvey; Chris Perry; Mildred D. Trask; Steve Bradbury; Mary Jane Wormstead; Barbara Lawrence; Elizabeth Duffill; Robert Spofford of the Massachusetts Firefighters Academy; Joseph R. Sousa and the East Greenwich, Rhode Island Veteran Firemen's Association, Inc.; Eugene I. Morris and the New England Fire & History Museum in Brewster, Massachusetts; William Travers, David Benner, Chris Perry, Harry Pinkham and the Waldoborough Historical Society, Waldoboro, Maine; Charles Maurais; Mollie Taylor; the Danvers Historical Society, and the Danvers Archival Center.

Gardner S. Trask, Sr. stands at far right in the driveway of fire headquarters in this 1948 photo of Engine 4.

INTRODUCTION

Looking Back: The Early History of Firefighting in Danvers

BY
RICHARD B. TRASK

What youngster has never daydreamed of being a firefighter? As a boy born within the post-World War II baby boom generation, my childhood playthings included a stuffed "Smokey the Bear," a red straw fireman's helmet, *The Great Big Fire Engine Book,* numerous metal and plastic toy fire trucks, and an awesome pedal-powered fire engine in which I could sit and scurry around the neighborhood. I had another thing going for me in my daydreams of being a firefighter—my dad was a Danvers Call Fireman. Gardner S. Trask, Sr., besides being a Boston banker, also lived a life of comradeship, excitement and volunteerism in the Danvers Fire Department which he had joined as a call fireman in late 1940. His service was interrupted for the Navy during World War II, and then reactivated in January 1946.

In his younger days during the 1930s Gardner, upon hearing the whistle at Central Fire Station, would run from his house on Chase Street to Bayview Avenue to hitch a ride with Joe Kelley and his dad the Fire Chief, for a chance to help out at a fire. Much later, in 1951, on his responding to an alarm as a call fireman in his car equipped with a blinking red light, my father suffered a severe heart attack that put him out of service for three months. He joyfully returned to "House Duty" for two months and then was assigned to Truck 5. Until his death in a train crash in February 1956, my father was always fervently interested in the department and its men. He was honored by his friends in death, and my brother Gardner and I had emblazoned into our minds the crepe-draped Central Fire Station and the ladder truck being used as flower car at his funeral.

My favorite memories, however, are of going with him Saturday mornings to the Central Fire Station or to Engine 3 to visit with his chums including Ray Guppy, Charlie Doyle, Phil Davis, Joe Kelley, Walt Skinner, Webby Dwinnell, Rollie Sturtevant, and Leland "Marty" Martin. I recall the mixed smells of drying hose, grease, cigar and pipe smoke, the sights of old sleds in the attic, and the white earthenware mugs used for coffee and the antique tin cups used as ash trays. It was thrilling for a youngster like me to be allowed to slide down the pole (never letting bare hands touch the polished surface). At the tender age of six I got to ride in an engine responding to an alarm at Danvers Park at "10:44 a.m., 11.15.53," as my father meticulously recorded in his personal log of fires.

Once to check my readiness as a potential firefighter, the guys at Central Fire Station rang the bells and hollered for me to get aboard the engine, just moments after I had leisurely entered the stall and sat upon the "head" in the back of the station. I also remember being so proud to get to ride in the bucket seat of a pumper during a parade outside of Danvers amidst the bellowing cacophony of dozens of engine sirens and bells. I recall the occasional sad feelings when a comrade was injured responding to a fire, how upset my Dad was when he was one of several searchers looking for a lost man whom they found dead in the woods, or the time at a fire that I was hastily put in our car when a fire victim was discovered among the ashes.

Daydreaming aboard Engine No. 4 in the early 1950s.

Though my life as a "spark" waned after my father's passing, and his hitch was no longer ready beside his bed and the fire alarm bell in our cellar stairway was disconnected, my appreciation and respect for firefighters in general and the Danvers Fire Department in particular has never faded. I can well recall the many nights lying in bed in a state somewhere between consciousness and sleep when suddenly my mind was jolted to full reality by the mournful blasts of the fire whistle pulsating through the night air. Something akin to fear entered my heart as I realized that someone was possibly in peril at that very moment. A few moments later, however, the frightful, yet reassuring, shrieks of the fire trucks' sirens brought comfort in knowing that the speedy response of a professional fire department, equipped with the most advanced firefighting and life-saving devices, would soon be at the source of the alarm.

Time certainly has brought immense progress to the nation's fire departments, and the Danvers department has undergone numerous changes, improvements, and professional developments from the relatively short time of my youth in the 1950s until today. How many more changes are reflected in the almost two hundred years of history of the Danvers Fire Department. Two hundred years ago most communities had no firefighting equipment, save water buckets and muscle. Yet even with the advent of the volunteer fire companies and their hand-operated engines, fires would often level a structure, and sometimes get so out of control as to cause a major conflagration that would destroy numerous buildings.

The volunteer firefighters of the nineteenth century often joined the company primarily for social reasons, and more than once, company rivalry would take precedence over fighting the fire. Yet this period from about 1800 to 1900 of the volunteer firefighter and his hand-operated engine is one of the most romantic and interesting ones in the social history of this nation. It was a time when men and muscles occasionally dueled with their fascinating rival—fire; and shared excitement and good comradeship with their company. The following pages of introduction tell the story of these volunteer fire companies of Danvers. In so doing the story will in part dwell upon the history of firefighting in general, for although such an average community as the Danvers, Massachusetts, of the 1800s cannot have as spectacular a fire department's history as that of the large cities of the nation, it does reflect what happened in most American communities and to the development of firefighting in general.

The Danvers, Massachusetts, of 1800 was larger in area than the present town, since within its boundaries was included the present-day city of Peabody, which in 1855 split off into the independent town of South Danvers. Containing a total area of about twenty-seven square miles, and twenty-six hundred inhabitants, Danvers was experiencing growing pains at the advent of the nineteenth century.

This ornately painted Fulton Fire Club leather bucket, including its owner's name, is typical of the pair of buckets each club member hung in his home ready for action.

With the population rising steadily each year from 1800 so that by 1840 it had about doubled, as well as growth in building new residences and businesses in newly occupied areas of town, the Danvers selectmen realized that the danger of fire grew ever more prevalent. The old unorganized bucket brigades were sufficient for small fires, but should a water supply be too distant, or the discovery of a blaze too slow, a fire was virtually free to consume anything in its path.

Like other communities in Massachusetts, Danvers was divided into several pocket villages, the most important ones at the beginning of the nineteenth century being at South Danvers and New Mills (now Danversport). Thus it was that on August 25, 1800, two hand-operated fire engines were voted to be purchased by the town with one half of the sum raised by subscription. The *Federal* Engine Company No. 1 was located near the Bell Tavern in the commercial district of the South Parish, while *Danvers* Engine Company No. 2 was set up in New Mills. Both of these "receiving engines" were built by Ephraim & Stephen Thayer of Boston and their mechanisms required water to be bucketed into their tubs. Men would then pump the water out onto the fire through a metal pipe sticking out the other end of the Engine.[1]

In May 1821 the town purchased two additional engines from Hunneman & Co. of Boston for $500. Delivered on July 10, 1822, the *Niagara* No. 1 replaced the *Federal* in the South Parish. This new engine was eventually moved to what is now West Peabody in the 1860s and sold in 1869. The other Hunneman engine, *Danvers* No. 2, apparently replaced the old Thayer apparatus at New Mills.[2]

An adjunct to the engine companies which served a useful function in the community was the fire club. Before the advent of the fire engine, bucket brigades had performed the necessary task of fighting fires. The fire club was an extension of these old bucket brigades, though these clubs were also social in nature. The Columbian Fire Club was established in 1804, while the Franklin Fire Club was instituted in 1821. The Fulton Fire Club was constituted in 1826 at New Mills with the following preamble to its constitution:

> We, the subscribers, believing that important advantages result from the institution of Fire Clubs, both to the community generally and to the individuals associated, and that we may the more effectually aid each other and those around us, and to promote harmony and good fellowship among ourselves form into a society, by the name of the Fulton Fire Club.[3]

Restricted to a membership of thirty-two and elected by unanimous vote, those in the club were the most prominent men in their section of town. Each member, according to the constitution, "shall procure and keep two buckets, a bag and a bed screw [for taking apart a bed]....This fire apparatus shall be kept in a conspicuous part of his dwelling, in readiness and good order, to be used as occasion may require. The buckets and bag shall be marked with the device of the club, and the name of the owner."[4] Among other fire memorabilia, the Danvers Historical Society has five of these leather fire buckets.

Article V of the Fulton Fire Club explained what to do in case of fire:

> On notice of fire each member, whose property is not in danger, shall immediately proceed with his buckets and bag to the building most in danger; and under the direction of the committee, or the member whose property is exposed, if present, shall faithfully endeavour to secure all his effects, both from the power of the fire and hazard of pillage, and in case of the removal of his effects shall assist in returning them to him again free of expense. And it shall be the duty of every member to take particular care of the goods and effects of any member, which may be exposed in his absence. For neglect of any part of the duty enjoined in this article, unless a satisfactory excuse is given the committee, the penalty shall be two dollars.
>
> After the fire has ceased, and the danger from it is no longer apprehended, it shall be the duty of the members, to meet at such place as they may be directed by the officers of the Club, and there remain until the roll has been called and the Club dismissed. Any member that shall have been present during the fire, and shall not answer to his name at the calling of the roll, shall be fined twenty-five cents.[5]

Electing officers, giving secret watch words, collecting fines for all sorts of misdemeanors, and having sumptuous meals and not too little drink, the fire club was also quite social in makeup.

Records of Danvers Town Meeting and of the engine companies themselves show that the Town had an organized volunteer fire department with elected firewards and appointed enginemen from 1801. It was not until March 1830, however, that an act to establish a fire department in Danvers was passed in the Massachusetts General Court. The act read in part:

> Sec. 1. Be it enacted by the Senate and House of Representatives in General Court assembled, and by the authority of the same, That the Inhabitants of the Town of Danvers, at their annual meeting for the

choice of Town Officers shall choose by ballot, twelve persons as
Firewards in said Town.

Sec. 3. Be it further enacted, That the said Firewards be, and they
are hereby authorized, if they shall judge it expedient, to nominate and
appoint, any number of Enginemen, in addition to the number now
authorized by law, not exceeding in the whole, forty men for each and
every hydraulion, or suction Engine, four men to each Hose Carriage,
twenty men to each Sail Carriage, and twenty men to be employed as a
Hook and Ladder Company, and the said Enginemen are authorized to
organize themselves into distinct companies, under the direction of the
Firewards: to elect directors, clerks, and other officers; to establish
such rules and regulations as may be approved by the Firewards, and
to annex penalties to the same which may be recovered by the Clerk of
any company so organized, before any Justice of the Peace in the
County of Essex: Provided, that no penalty shall exceed the sum of ten
dollars; and that such rules and regulations shall not be repugnant to
the Constitution and laws of this Commonwealth.

Sec. 4. Be it further enacted, That the said Firewards shall have the
care and superintendence of the public Pumps, and Cisterns, and also
of the public Engines, Hose, and Sail Carriages, Fire Hooks, and
Ladders, together with the buildings, fixtures, and appendages, thereto
belonging and shall cause the same to be kept in good repair; and may
from time to time, make such alterations and improvements, there in,
as they shall deem expedient: Provided that the sums expended for
such repairs, alterations, and improvements shall not exceed in any one
year the sum of one-hundred dollars, unless the said Town of Danvers
shall have previously assented to a larger appropriation.[6]

The fire department now had a specifically structured organization, and yearly regulations for the Fire Department were printed beginning in 1831.

After 1830, at the annual election of town officials, twelve firewards were chosen. At the first meeting of the Board of Firewards, these dozen men chose from among themselves a Chief Engineer, Secretary, and five Assistant Engineers who became the Board of Engineers. The Chief Engineer presided over the monthly and special meetings of the Board of Engineers and Firewards, and was in charge of the entire Department, much like the Fire Chief of today's department. Upon the absence of the Chief Engineer, the First Assistant Engineer became acting Chief Engineer. The Secretary was responsible for keeping the records of the meetings of the Board of Engineers and Firewards.

Men assigned to the various engine companies of the town had to be approved and appointed by the Board of Firewards, and were given a certificate assigning them to a volunteer company and entitling them to the privileges and exemptions that enginemen received. The certificate could be revoked because of misconduct, and each year the appointment had to be renewed.

The Board of Firewards assigned themselves so that each engine company had a fireward attached to it. The engine company fireward was to supervise the work of the engine company at a fire, and directed them when to return or not to go to a fire. Sub-committees, which were responsible for the repair and maintenance of the engines, engine houses, equipment, pumps and cisterns, were formed from among the Board of Engineers and Firewards.[7]

As customs developed, the favorite or most respected member of the engine company was usually asked to run for the position of fireward in the annual election; and, with the votes of his company behind him, he seldom lost and was able to be on the lookout for the best interests of his company. Thus it was that engine companies were often stepping stones to an office within the fire department, and eventually to other posts within town government. In large cities many political aspirants got their start within a volunteer fire company as was the case with the famous William "Boss" Tweed of New York.

Besides the organization of the Board of Engineers and Firewards, the individual engine companies also had an organization of responsibility. In May of each year the individual members of the company chose by ballot a first, second, and third Director, and Clerk. The First Director presided at all company meetings and directed all operations of the company subject to the firewards. In his absence, the duties were taken over by the Second Director. The Clerk was to take down the minutes of the monthly or special meetings of the company, collect fines, and act as treasurer. He was also to record fires sounded, and the amount of time the engine was absent from the engine house.

The number of engine companies saw fast growth during the 1830s and 1840s. In the spring of 1830 a new Hunneman & Co. suction engine was obtained by the town, named *Torrent* No. 3, and placed into service in the South Parish on Central Street. During the first half of the decade Danvers' New Mills engine changed its name several times by vote of the company from *Erie* to *Reformer* to *Albion*. Between 1836 and 1837 Danvers obtained two new engines, these built by Samuel Huse & Co. of Newburyport. Danvers Plains was fast developing as a community center of the North Parish and successful agitation was made by its citizens for a "new" engine there. The *General Putnam* No. 4 was a $750 piece of apparatus. The contract between Huse and the town dated July 5, 1836, described its specifications:

> The pumps of said Engine to be seven & three quarter inches in Diameter with Plungers to move eleven inches. The tub to be of copper. Sides not less than 40 oz. Bottom 60 oz. The motion of the breaks to be horizontal. The Engine to be capable of throwing as much water as any other Engine of the same capacity or dimention. To be well built in a good & substantial manner with two pipes & two outlets for throwing two separate streams of water at the same time. Also to be furnished with twenty-eight feet Rileys Best Suction Hose 3/4 inches in diameter. The cylinders, water ways & screws to be of composition. The wheels to be well made & heavy brass mounted. The Engine to be well painted & fitted in every respect for use & for a first rate article. With all necessary apparatus usually required for a fire Engine.[8]

It appears that Huse & Co. had earlier provided Danvers with a trial engine, "which we had offered at a very low price." This too was acquired by the town at a cost of $575 and named *Eagle* No. 5 for use in the South Parish.

Built in 1830 for Danvers and named **Torrent No. 3,** *this Hunneman & Company engine was later sold by the town to a Maine community and renamed* **Medomak.** *It is now part of the collection of the Waldoborough Historical Society in Maine.*

By early 1844 the town again saw the need for establishing new fire companies, and on March 1, 1844, Edward S. Lesley of Newburyport delivered to Danvers two new 6" cylinder engines at a cost of $1588. The relatively new village in the North Parish known as Tapley's Village (later Tapleyville) also pressured for a piece of apparatus. It did not receive a new engine, however, but rather the Company No. 2 engine dating from 1822 originally placed at New Mills, was transferred to Tapley's Village and renamed *General Scott* No. 2. New Mills received one of the new Lesley engines, which was given the name *Ocean* No. 6. The second new engine was named *General Foster* No. 7, named after Danvers Revolutionary War hero Gideon Foster, and located on Lowell Street in the South Parish.[9]

From the 1830s through the 1860s the organization of the Fire Department remained essentially the same. By 1844, Danvers had seven engines compared to the two in 1800. Other apparatus also became permanent fixtures within the department. An 1844 broadside on fire department regulations listed the following "Location of Engines, Sail Carriages, and Hooks and Ladders":

Edward Lesley of Newburyport certifies in 1844 the delivery of two new engines soon to be named Ocean *and* General Foster.

Engines:
Engine No. 1, near Wm. Suttons Brick store, Main Street
Engine No. 2, Tapley's Village
Engine No. 3, Central Street
Engine No. 4, At the Plains
Engine No. 5, At the Sign of the Eagle, Main Street
Engine No. 6, New Mills
Engine No. 7, Lowell Street

Sail Carriages:
One at No. 5 Engine House
One at No. 6 Engine House

Hooks and Ladders:
Main Street, near Hamblet's Store
Main Street, on Carter & Batchelder's Store
Washington Street, near J. Morrison's House
Engine House No. 5
Near K. Osborn's Store
Foster Street, on A. Torr's Bark House

Central Street, Opposite Engine House No. 3
At the Neck - rear of Baptist Meeting House
At the Neck - on Fox Hill
Plains - near Berry's Stable [10]

Beside the locations of the apparatus, the broadside also listed twenty-three public pumps, plugs and cisterns located in various parts of town that were used as a water supply during a fire. Individuals could petition the firewards for construction of a cistern if they felt that water was unavailable in their area and they were unprotected in case of fire.

The following is an excerpt of a typical fireward committee's investigation of a petition for a reservoir:

> The committee would state that they have examined this subject, and that they entertain the opinion that a good well or reservoir is needed in this vicinity, which would furnish a supply of water for Elm and Central Streets in case of fires. We believe there is no well or cistern in this vicinity capable of furnishing a supply of water for our Engine, but a very short time....We would suggest that a large and capacious well might be dug on Central Street, from which the water could be taken by an engine whenever needed at an expense of about one-hundred dollars, or a Reservoir capable of holding six-thousand or more gallons of water and warranted perfectly tight could be constructed by the side of the well at an additional expense of about two-hundred dollars....[11]

After the Town Meeting heard the firewards' recommendations, they voted on it. Almost always a petition for construction of a water supply was favorably reported and voted on, since everyone recognized the danger of fire.

The seven town engines were almost always attended by hose reels or carts. These reels carried leather hose, usually about six-hundred feet, and could be either drawn separately, or hauled attached to the engine's tail hook. Although there were four-wheeled varieties, most of the hose reels used in Danvers were of the two-wheel type. The sail carriages carried canvas that was used in a variety of ways, including for the smothering of small fires. The hooks and ladders were not separate vehicles until the late 1840s in larger cities, and much later in Danvers. The hooks were attached to long sturdy poles and used for tearing walls down to either stop the spread of fire or destroy burning walls already afire. The hooks and ladders were placed in key locations throughout town so that when a fire broke out, a few men would run to where they were located and carry them back to the scene of the fire. Often these hooks and ladders were stored in long, narrow shelters built at convenient intervals along the road.[12]

Those men attached to the engine companies were assigned a specific task to perform. Leading hose men would "play the pipe" (direct the stream of water from the nozzle onto the fire); suction hose men would position the suction hose into a water supply in order to draw water; and brakemen would manually operate the rods or bars by which the hand-pumped engine would suck in and spew out the water. Two axe men were also assigned to each engine.

The 1844 fire department regulations broadside listing seven engines in Danvers was barely off the press before the department again expanded. Prominent South Parish businessman General William Sutton volunteered the use of a New York manufactured L. Button side stroke-engine for a ten year period. Dubbed *Volunteer* No. 8, this apparatus was conveniently located near Sutton's brick store on Main Street next to Engine No. 1. By 1846 the *Volunteer* was located right next to the Sutton store, while No. 1 was placed with No. 5 farther up Main Street "at the sign of the Eagle."

During street work in June 1986 an old fire department water cistern was temporarily uncovered at Maple and Hobart Street.

In 1849 the nineteen-year-old *Torrent* No. 3 engine in the South Parish was replaced by a new Hunneman & Co., Boston manufactured 6 1/8" cylinder engine. The new engine kept the name "Torrent." The old 1822 *General Scott* No. 2 engine housed at Tapley's Village was sold in 1850 for $210 and was replaced by a new Lesley 6 1/2" cylinder end stroke machine which arrived in March 1850 costing, with credit for the old engine, $653.37.

Prior to the separation of Danvers and South Danvers in 1855, the last major change involving engines occurred in December 1854, when a new *Volunteer* No. 8 was purchased by the town to replace the engine General Sutton had loaned to the town for a decade. The new engine was manufactured by L. Button & Co. and was able to handle the power of thirty-two brakemen. It cost $1,100, with a brass mounted hose cart and three hundred ninety-six feet of single riveted hose adding $421.60 to the cost.[13]

By far the most important piece of equipment which the town's fire department possessed, and the one with which the firemen most identified, was the engine. The engine was looked upon by her men as an entity unto herself and was the focal point of pride in the volunteer companies. Along with this immense pride in their engine came rivalry among the various fire companies. At the sound of an alarm the men would run to their engine house, pick up the drag ropes and pull their engine as quickly as possible to the fire, often not so much to get to the fire fast, but to beat all the other kits to the scene of action.

There were several types of hand-operated fire engines such as the "gooseneck," "Philadelphia," "piano box," and "crane-neck" styles. The general principle of operation was the same, however. A suction hose was immersed into a water supply and the water was sucked into the engine's air chamber and then forced out by cylinder action. The forcing in and flowing out of water was accomplished by the brakemen who manually operated the brakes in an up-and-down motion forcing water into the chamber, then out through the eduction pipe, through the lengths of leather hose, and on through the brass pipe (nozzle). A stroke consisted of a full up-and-down motion of the brakes, and the usual stroke rate was about sixty per minute. At this pace, a steady and powerful stream of

In 1849 the old **Torrent No. 3** *was replaced in the South Parish by this new Hunneman engine. It remained in what became the town of Peabody until 1882.*

water flowed from the pipe and a brakeman could work the brakes for about fifteen minutes. Often, however, at a serious fire the stroke rate went over one hundred twenty strokes a minute, and the brakeman who had helped to pull his heavy engine to the fire at top speed lasted only a few minutes at the brakes. Often, too, men would receive broken fingers or arms when jumping in to relieve someone at the brakes, and not catching the fast-moving bar at the right moment.

On September 6, 1847, a fire totally destroyed the Baptist Church on Water Street. Shortly thereafter an article appeared in the *Danvers Courier* which spoke of the job of the engineman and about the uncooperativeness of some spectators.

> At the recent fire at New Mills, we were surprised at the conduct of several well, able-bodied men, who refused to lend their assistance in relieving the engine men, some of whom had dragged their engines for several miles, and exerted themselves at the brakes for some half hour in addition. Now it should be remembered by all those who at every fire volunteer their services to lounge around, look on or get themselves in the way of those who are at work, that engine men are made of the same material that other men are, and although they are paid one shilling an hour for their services—which will only replace the amount of clothing destroyed in performing their duty—they still need like most other men a few minutes rest after exerting themselves to their utmost for an hour or two. Although it may be an unpleasant duty of the Fireward to compel these lazy drones to do some service, we hope they will not in future excuse or spare them.[14]

If the scene of the fire was too far away from a water supply, the first engine company on the scene would put its suction hose into the water, lay a hose line

Built in 1854, the **Volunteer** *eventually saw fire service in Peabody; Derry, New Hampshire; and Central Falls, Rhode Island. It was purchased in 1913 by the East Greenwich (R.I.) Veteran Firemen's Association and continues to be used in muster competitions.*

as far as it could while still able to maintain water pressure, and upon arrival of the next engine would cry, "Will you take our water?" The second engine would set up next to the first engine's extended hose and take this water received from the pumping of the first engine as its suction source. Thus the first engine's water would be pumped into the second engine, through the chamber, and out its hose. If the water supply was a distance away from the fire, a long line of engines would be needed to relay one stream of water onto the fire. If this was the case, valuable time was lost in setting up the relay, and even then only one stream could play upon the flames.

Even in such a serious circumstance as a relay, the fire companies tried to out-rival one another. If an engine was fed more water than her brakemen could stroke out of her chamber, water would flood over the engine and onto the ground, soaking the brakemen and signifying that her men were not strong and fast enough to pump out the water received from another engine. Thus if such a "washing" took place, the company that was washed was in disgrace and subject to the taunts of other companies. To a fireman this was the ultimate embarrassment, and their engine could no longer be referred to as a "virgin."

In July 1845 a typical trial of engines took place between *Eagle* and *Gen. Foster* Companies whereby the *Foster* was to attempt to "run over" the *Eagle* with water while the *Eagle* strove to pump off the water received through another length of hose. Although the contest was to run for ten minutes, at the seventh minute the *Eagle* fractured one of her brakes, and the contest was decided in favor of the *Foster*. Another engine, the *Volunteer*, had supplied the *Foster* with water, "very handsomely, making the ground somewhat damp around the latter engine," as the *Courier* newspaper correspondent quite cutely reported.[15]

As previously noted, the first step in procuring a new fire engine for a section of town was often by citizen petition. This 1830 petition for what would eventually be the *Torrent* engine is typical:

> To the Selectmen of the Town of Danvers. Gentlemen, you are requested to insert a clause in the town warrant at the next annual March meetings - to see if Town will provide another Fire Engine, with a suction hose to the same, to be located near the South meeting House.[16]

This petition was signed by twenty-six prominent men from that section of town. Thereupon a committee was appointed by the town to look into the matter of a new engine. The March 29, 1830, findings of the committee read:

> We are of opinion that it would be best to procure an Hydraulion engine, with suction hose, and such a quantity of leading hose, as will be necessary for the convenient operation of the same. The expense of procuring such an engine, hose and hose carriages, will probably be not less that $800 nor more than $1,000. We have examined the Engine House belonging to the Town and think it would be sufficiently large to accommodate another engine.[17]

According to its engine company record book, Company No. 1 began having trouble with its apparatus "coincidentally" only a few months before the town was to purchase two new engines, which various sections of town hoped to acquire for their area. On October 1, 1821, the "Engine Company met at engine house fill'd and discharged the engine found all in order." One month later, however, the engine was described as "a poor old thing," though it had not seen any action since the previous month's tryout. By April 1822, the engine was "much out of order," and in May it was characterized as "a disgraceful old thing." June found the engine in "miserable order." Engine Company No. 1 got its new apparatus in July.[18]

When a fire company either purchased its first engine or a new one to replace an outdated model, that engine typically arrived in town without adornment, painted lead gray, and covered with grease. The firemen would try out the new engine by discharging her a few times, pulling her to get the feel, and generally satisfying themselves as to her capacity. If the engine company, the firewards, and the selectmen were satisfied, the vehicle would become part of the town's fire department.

Soon after the new engine's arrival, she would be painted and decorated, usually at the expense of the volunteers. This was important to the men, for in order to be the prestigious symbol of the company, the engine must look good. After the painting was completed, fancy brass ornaments would be added, and an appropriate name given to the engine. As of 1855 Danvers' engines were known by: *Niagara* (No. 1), *General Scott* (No. 2), *Torrent* (No. 3), *General Putnam* (No. 4), *Eagle* (No. 5), *Ocean* (No. 6), *General Foster* (No. 7), and *Volunteer* (No. 8).

Usually engine record book entries are very brief and to the point, but in the August 1850 monthly report for Engine No. 6, clerk Maurice C. Oby gives us a nice glimpse of how the men regarded their machine.

> The Company met agreeably to the notice given at 7 o'clock p.m. proceeded to work the Engine immediately after roll call. The personal appearance of Oceane the green of water nymphs, was beautiful to behold, having been lately blacked and varnished, and her numerous ornaments of Brass, cleaned and polished in the best manner, she shone and glittered like a gaily dressed Belle at a country Ball. On trial with water through a 3/4 inch pipe she threw at least 5 feet higher than the vane of the steeple of the Baptist House at New Mills which is 110 feet high. The suction power and her capacity for passing a dense stream of water without air or wind proves her virgin vigor to be as yet unimpaired by service or other usage. Indeed she was in admirable condition, and her performance of water works on this occasion was a worthy tribute to her noble name.[19]

In an average Danvers volunteer fire company during the 1830s through the 1860s, there were usually about fifty or sixty volunteers attached to each engine house. Besides the social gains which a fireman would be able to enjoy, he was exempt from a military draft, should any take place, and exempt from paying poll taxes. But even with these privileges, a fireman still had many perils to offset his gains. Fines ranging from twelve to seventy-five cents were taken against firemen who did not run to the station on the sounding of an alarm, or were not on hand for the roll call after a fire. Missing monthly meetings also brought on a fine as did unmanly conduct during a fire. To have one's certificate invalidated because of misconduct was a disgrace hard to shake. So, too, while running to a fire one might stumble and be run over by the immense weight of the engine, or the firefighter might receive broken bones while operating the brakes. But in spite of these hazards many men wanted to join a fire company in order to partake in the social pleasures it inspired and the heroic comradeship it gave.

At appointed times throughout the year, the company would gather to work the engine to see if it and the equipment functioned properly. In the winter months, a member of the company would be given the responsibility "...to keep the snow and all other obstructions from the doors of the engine house." Someone was also responsible for putting sled runners on the engine when the snow precluded the running of the engines on their wheels.

Exact records of time spent with the engine outside the engine house were kept by the company clerk, for each man received "one shilling per hour, for the

Broadside by-laws printed in 1845 for Ocean No. 6, the engine located in Danversport.

time he shall spend in the performance of his duty as a member of the Department..."[20] This pay did not amount to much, however, especially after fines were deducted. Often men completed the year having given more money in fines than having received in pay.

According to the written duties of volunteers, when a fire ocurred, "Enginemen, duly appointed, are held and obliged to go forward, either by night or by day, under the direction of the Firewards, in the same town, and to use their best endeavors to extinguish any fire that may happen in the same town or in the vicinity thereof, that shall come to their knowledge, without delay."[21]

Most fires were discovered by the smoke in the daytime air or by the glow of the flames at night, since little else was in the sky to distract an observer. Thus even fairly minor fires were able to be detected if one was looking in the right direction.

Those who saw a fire were obliged to scream "FIRE" until someone could get a key to a meetinghouse and begin to ring the church bell, which would in turn signal a response from other meetinghouse bells. In the record book of Engine No. 2, it was noted on September 5, 1835: "There be a committee of two chosen to wait on the committee of the Baptist society to see if the key of the Baptist meeting house can be left where the members of the engine company can

find it in case of fire." Earlier, in 1813, the South Meetinghouse offered a $20 reward for detecting the culprit who had repeatedly stolen the tongue of the church bell, as that person disrupted church life and the public notification of fires. [22]

Once a fire alarm was ringing, the volunteers would drop whatever they were doing and run to the engine house. If the fire was out of town or at a very great distance, the first men to arrive with two horses would have them hitched to the engine, and the volunteers would follow the engine and horse to the fire, not being allowed to ride on the engine. A reward of twenty-five cents plus twenty-five cents per mile would be given to the owners of the horses for letting them be used by the company. [23]

If the fire was in town, however, the men would pull the engine themselves, since it was a point of pride to so do in one's own town. They would also race other engines to the fire to prove their company's strength and agility. When enough men arrived at the engine house so that the heavy machine could be moved, the officer in charge would holler, "Start her lively, boys!" and the engine would be jerked to a fast start. As more men ran up to the moving vehicle, they would grab hold of the drag ropes and pull for all they were worth. Others would rush for the hooks and ladders, and often someone would speedily carry a cask of liquor to the scene of the fire for a stimulating incentive to the brakemen at work.

On occasion the engine would mistakenly go the wrong way and lose much valuable time finding the fire. On March 8, 1845, Engine No. 6 "...by mistake proceeded up High Street" while going to a Salem fire, and arrived too late to assist. [24]

A drawing by David S. Shattuck of the Maple Street Congregational Church at Danvers Plains which was burned in 1850. The replacement church built on this site was also destroyed by a fire in 1944.

A fairly rich account of a fire at Danvers Plains was written in the record book of Engine No. 6 for July 10, 1850.

> Fire broke out of the Congregational Society House at Danvers Plains a few minutes before eleven o'clock p.m. which soon became a ruin, undoubtedly the work of an incendiary, loss estimated at about 7,000 Dols. insured for 4,000 Dols. Precisely at 11 o'clock the alarm was given for the *Ocean* to get in motion, which was whirled with great dispatch to the fire. The engine located first at the cistern opposite the meeting house, afterwards at the one near the Bank where we drafted and forced water for a line of 5 engines and worked admirably, giving them far more water from the *Ocean* that they could dispose of at least to their satisfaction.[25]

Often at a large fire neighbors would bring refreshments to the tired firemen. This was done at the church fire, and duly noted in the record book.

> The Company tender their hearty thanks to John Page, Perly and Company and others for the bountiful supply of refreshments provided them at the late fire. Voted that the clerk cause a card to the above purport to be inserted in the *Essex Freeman* and *Salem Observer*.

As an interesting sidelight to this fire, two boys had set it. One of the boys helped work the brakes of the *General Putnam* to put out the fire, and he was later proposed for company membership - and accepted. The other boy confessed to having set the fire, and he was sentenced and served ten years in Charlestown Jail for the crime of arson. [26]

Human tragedies, including the loss of life, were constant companions of fire. On March 11, 1856, one such incident was recorded in a company book.

Alarm of Fire

> Originated from the burning of the two story wooden house of F. Gould at Danversport, the house was occupied by 4 Irish families, and all but one man, by name Daniel O'Breen, escaped with their life from the burning house; it hardly seems possible that in a chamber about 10 feet from the ground; at that angle of the house which was most distant from the little kitchen where the fire took and commenced, that a healthy middle aged man, whose wife and child escapes safely from the same bed should have been burnt up alive. But such was the fact, - and will long be remembered, perhaps had not the whole body of men & women who belonged to the house been so frightened and crazed, he would have been saved. The alarm commenced at half past eleven p.m. Nov. 11th and from some cause or other it was scarcely heard off the place. No other Engine but 4 of the Plains took the alarm and that had hardly 10 members of its company with it. The rest were sleeping. Fortunately from the direction of the wind, and the fact that the

Ocean's hose just reached from the cistern; and the good exertions of all, the fire was confined to one house, and an extensive conflagration prevented.[27]

The rapid growth of the Danvers Fire Department between the late 1830s and mid 1840s is due to the construction boom in Danvers and also to the devastation caused by several major conflagrations. In the early morning hours of September 22, 1843, a fire began in the business district of the South Parish. Fed by gale-force winds, the fire spread quickly from the William Berry wheelwright shop, eventually destroying over fourteen major buildings including the new South Church, then under construction. An estimated $75,000 damage was done to this thriving commercial area.[28]

The Plains village of Danvers would evolve in size and prominence to become the most important commercial area in North Danvers. This area is today known as Danvers Square. In the 1830s, however, the village, which had begun with but two stores and a few scattered dwellings, had between thirty and forty structures located there.

By 1845 the Plains was well-established and a prospering area. Engine No. 4 was stationed on Maple Street, adjacent to the Congregational Church. Named after Danvers' Revolutionary War hero, General Israel Putnam, the company had a complement of about forty-five volunteers. Hooks and ladders were kept in the ready near the Berry Tavern stables on the southeastern end of the square nearest to the road to Salem. Two cisterns were located at the Plains, one near J. A. Learoyd's house and the other between the Village Bank and J. Silvester's shoe shop.

June of 1845 was a very hot and dry month with daily temperatures rising past the one hundred degree mark. The first half of the month saw an unusual number of fires breaking out, which with water becoming scarce, alarmed the firewards as to the dangerous possibility of a major conflagration.

Then, on June 10, at about 1:45 p.m. it happened. According to a newspaper account of the fire:

> The cause is not known with certainty; but it broke out in an outbuilding belonging to the dwelling house of Mr. Joshua Silvester, and was said to have been occasioned by some children playing with friction matches. The fire spread with great rapidity and seemed at one time beyond human control.[29]

More than likely the first engine on the spot was the *General Putnam*. Soon the Maple Street Church bell was clanging the alarm, to be echoed a few minutes later by the other bells in Danvers Centre and Danversport. The fire spread quickly through the buildings on the west side of the Square. The other engines in various parts of town "took to the ropes" and pulled hard and fast for the scene.

As the fire became furiously out of control and continued to consume new buildings, crowds of townspeople ran to the scene and began to help salvage property. Some manned bucket brigades which tried to prevent small fires being touched off by burning embers, into becoming larger fires. The water supply was helplessly low. If the cisterns had done any good during the initial stages of the fire, the supply was soon depleted, and now the nearest body of water was Frost Fish Brook, half a mile away from the fire. It was necessary to hook up a row of eight engines in order to pump the water to the fire and still maintain effective water pressure. Thus eight engines were needed to produce a single stream of water onto the conflagration. Realizing the danger of this fire, no engine company engaged in such sport as trying to "wash" another engine, but all the men strained at the brakes, now going well over one-hundred strokes a minute. This work was hard enough, but coupled with the immense heat of the day, the work was inhumanly tiring. A man could last only a few minutes at the brakes before having to be relieved.

> The alarm reached Salem at about a quarter past 2 and several engines and fire companies immediately started, guided by the direction of the smoke, although it was not then known where the fire was, nor how imminent was the danger. Express messengers arrived some time afterwards for assistance, when the alarm was again sounded, and several more engines were dispatched, making seven in all from Salem, preceded, accompanied, and followed by great numbers of citizens. The progress over the length of dusty road was exceedingly toilsome, with the utmost vertical sun beating down upon their unsheltered heads at a temperature of 120 degrees to 130 degrees. Some were much overcome by the exposure and fatigue. [30]

According to recollections later shared by *General Foster* engine company Second Director W. J. C. Kennedy:

> This company was stationed during the fire near Mr. Amos Brown's house. While getting here across from the square the heat was so intense that only six men went with the engine and Mr. Kenney was very badly burned on his neck and the whole of one of his arms. He retired from the fire for a brief time while his neck and arm was covered with molasses brought from the store of Mr. Daniel Richards, by his son George. Mr. Kenney afterwards returned to his company, and the heat becoming so intense, two men held a barn door between the fire and the engine so that the men might work and be shielded somewhat from the heat of the fire. Those who remained, finally drew the engine out from the fire and thus saved it from destruction. Owing to the intense heat of the day, the men worked in their shirt sleeves. [31]

The flames were so intense and the sparks so plentiful that the fire jumped over to the east side of Maple Street, and began to consume buildings on that side. The *Danvers Courier* reported: "Those attached to the *Ocean*, No. 6 protected themselves and the man with the pipe by holding up a carpet as a shield against the fire without which no living being could have approached so near it." [32]

Six hours after it had begun, the fire had just about burned itself out. A total of eighteen buildings were destroyed, valued at $80,000, though only insured for

This ca. 1859 view of Danvers Square looks up Maple Street from near the corner of Conant Street. After the devastating 1845 fire, Maple Street was widened to prevent a future fire from jumping the street. The view shows what is most likely the 1837 S. Huse & Co. engine, **General Putnam No. 4,** *near the site of a large water cistern located under the road.*

$30,000. Seventeen engines had fought the fire including kits from Salem and Beverly.

Two days later on Thursday, June 12, another fire broke out in North Danvers destroying a barn and other outbuildings belonging to Israel Boardman. The next day a large fire in Tapley's Village brought the response of all town engines. A box, peg, and carpet factory was destroyed at the value of $11,000. Engine No. 2 was almost entirely consumed in the fire. That same day Engine Company No. 6 voted, "That 54 cts. be paid from the funds of the company for lemonade."[33] The hot, dry weather of the first half of June 1845 would not soon be forgotten.

As a result of the Plains fire, a new large brick cistern was built on the corner of Hobart and Maple Streets, and the east side of Maple Street was widened to the degree that it is today, so that another fire could not jump the street. The destroyed Noyes Shoe Factory was replaced in 1845 with "a substantial brick building which will serve as a barrier to the progress of fire." This brick and slate roof building is at 32-34 Maple Street. [34]

Of importance only second to that of fighting a fire, was the social life of the volunteer enginemen. Company get-togethers were occasions for camaraderie, drinking, eating, and "chewing the fat."

Company record books give ample proof on virtually every page of the social character of a fire company. Likewise local newspapers recorded in detail social gatherings including torchlight parades, tests of engines, and suppers in which the various local companies participated, including large-scale meetings in October 1847 and February 1848. In January of 1849, all the fire companies got together for a lavish supper at the Universalist Church. On occasion uniforms and torches were purchased for parade use.

In October of 1856 a public celebration and reception was given to Danvers' famous son George Peabody, who had achieved international notoriety in banking, and was becoming well known for his philanthropy. Asked by the Committee on Arrangements if Engine No. 6 would join in the parade, the company reported that they considered it "inexpedient to join the procession at his reception." Only a few days later, however, on learning that "a collation for the Fire Department" was to be provided, the company voted to negate the previous vote and attend the parade.

An engraving showing part of the October 1856 George Peabody celebration parade passing the Lexington Battle Monument in South Danvers. The engine being pulled by its drag line is most probably **General Foster No. 7,** *which was purchased by Danvers in 1844, prior to the separation of Danvers and South Danvers in 1855.*

The company proceeded to hire horses to pull the engine and a band to march in front of it. Many of the enginemen had always wanted a uniform to go along with the badge which had previously been adopted at a cost of twenty-four cents each. They decided to put together a uniform consisting of a white collar turned inside a red shirt, with the top button of the shirt unbuttoned, a black neck handkerchief, dark pants, glazed caps, and a belt with the word *"Ocean"* painted upon it. [35]

Reporting on the Peabody reception of October 9, 1856, the clerk of the company wrote, "The Company attended this reception today, everything passed off satisfactorily with the exception perhaps, that the dinner provided for the Firemen did not quite meet with their expectations."[36]

A typical social get-together is noted in the Engine No. 1 record book for November 9, 1821. "Engine Company met at Capt. Batcheldor's Inn and partook of a very excellent supper, fines all collected and money all expended, the members after enjoying themselves in innocent mirth dispersed in Friendship and brotherly love...." [37] A reading of the records of Engine No. 1, would make one wonder if they met more often in Batcheldor's Inn than in the Engine House.

Usually volunteer firemen were younger men, and when one died, the entire company would feel the loss and make appropriate resolutions such as the following one from the special meeting of Company No. 6 in November 1848:

The last hand pump engine Danvers acquired occurred in 1874 when a secondhand 1855 engine was purchased from Westfield, Massachusetts, for Danversport and named Ocean No. 3. *In June 1952 this former Danvers engine was displayed in Danvers' two hundredth anniversary parade.*

retained *General Scott* (No. 2 Tapleyville), *General Putnam* (No. 4 Plains), and *Ocean* (No. 6 Danversport); while South Danvers kept its five engines. By 1858 the Danvers companies reassigned numbers, with Engine No. 4 becoming No. 1, No. 2 staying the same, and No. 6 changing to No. 3. In 1872 the old 1837 *General Putnam* engine was sold and replaced by a double air chamber 10" cylinder engine manufactured by L. Button & Co.[43]

Steam-operated fire engines had been introduced in America in the 1850s, and were first purchased for use in the larger cities. The steam engine system essentially performed the same duty as the tiring, back-breaking work done by brakemen on the hand operated engines. Though a steam engine was much more expensive to purchase and needed the careful control of an engineer, it produced a steady source of water power at a fire and did not require a large complement of men. In 1866 a petition was submitted for town meeting action relating to the purchase of a steam engine for Danvers. A town committee reported to town meeting that among other problems, the purchase of a steam engine would cost $3,500, and that entirely new size hose would be needed at an added expense of $2,800. So, too, a larger fire house would be required to house the tall chimneyed engine at a cost of about $2,000. An estimated $940 would be necessary for the upkeep of the steam engine per year. The committee also felt that the acquisition of a steamer would only be able to replace one hand-operated engine and that the steamer would cause the department to double its budget. A negative recommendation was made. Most probably, the volunteer firefighters were also against the introduction of the steamer into the department, since it would take the place of almost all of the men in the company. Danvers Town Meeting voted to postpone action indefinitely. [44]

Two years later George W. Bell and others submitted another petition for town meeting action as regards to a steam fire engine. At this 1868 annual town meeting the controversial warrant article sparked heated debate. A hand vote indicated that the petition lost, but a requested poll of the voters showed that it carried by eighty to forty votes. This vote was also questioned and the moderator required supporters to step past him so he could physically tally the number. The final vote was seventy-six in favor to twenty-five against, though the vote was moot when no money was appropriated for its purchase. Several more years of controversy ensued. In the interim three self-acting extinguishers were purchased for the fire department's use. [45]

A late nineteenth century badge worn by the First Assistant of the Ocean *No. 3 hose company. Hose reels and wagons replaced the hand pump engines when Danvers established its piped water system.*

Danversport's 1844 *Ocean* No. 3 was replaced in 1874 by the purchase of a secondhand 1855 L. Button & Co. engine from Westfield Massachusetts, called *Rough and Ready*. Renamed *Ocean* No. 3, the single air chamber, 10" cylinder engine was sold by Danvers in 1878 and survived many years until destroyed in a New Hampshire fire in 1963.

Finally after money was grudgingly wrestled by a town meeting majority, in June 1874, *Danvers* No. 1 a second-class steam fire engine built by Hunneman and Co. of Boston, arrived in Danvers. The basement of Bell's Hall on Maple Street was outfitted for the apparatus, though the reign of a steam engine in town was short-lived.

Another controversial and expensive proposition debated in Danvers during the 1870s which had a major effect upon the fire department was the introduction of a piped municipal water system. After numerous meetings, studies, and heated debates, in 1875 the Danvers Water Act was enacted; and in 1876, twenty-one miles of street pipes were laid out and connected to Middleton Pond at a cost of $162,500. By the end of December the system was working and the water pressure through the pipes was strong enough to send a 1 3/8" stream of water some one-hundred twenty-five feet in the air. Suddenly all the Danvers suction hand engines and the steam engine were obsolete. The year 1877 saw the purchase of three hose carriages from Edward B. Leverick of New York at a cost of $250 each, and the establishment of eight hose companies and one hook and ladder company with a limit of eighty call firemen who would be available to serve the town in case of fire. [46]

By 1878 the Danvers hand engines were sold or for sale, and Holbrook, Massachusetts, purchased the Danvers steam engine for $2,025. With the advent of the municipal water system came the end of the rich social history of the large volunteer engine companies.

*In 1971 an old hose reel belonging to the **Matthew Hooper** Company No. 8 was rescued from an old barn in town. This reel was probably in use from 1877 till about 1883 at a time when the company was located at the Ironworks on Water Street. The apparatus is here examined by Thurl D. Brown and Richard B. Trask, who assisted in its recovery.*

BACK NOTES

1. *Danvers Town Meeting Record Book*, v. 5, p. 34.
2. *Ibid.*, v. 6, p. 229.
3. *Constitution and Laws of the Fulton Fire Club*, (Salem, W. & S. B. Ives, 1826), p. [3]; Hurd, D. Hamilton, comp. *History of Essex County, Massachusetts*, (Philadelphia, J. W. Lewis & Co., 1888), p. 498.
4. *Ibid.*, p. 4.
5. *Ibid.*, p. 6-7.
6. Danvers Fire Department manuscript records, "Act to establish a Danvers Fire Department," 1830.
7. Danvers Fire Department manuscript records, "Board of Fireward record books," 1830–1911.
8. Letter, Samuel Huse & Co. to Committee of Danvers Fire Department, July 5, 1836.
9. Letter, Edward S. Lesley to [Danvers], March 1, 1844; Hurd, op. cit., p. 499.
10. Danvers Fire Department, *Regulations Adopted By the Firewards of Danvers*, (Danvers, S. T. Damon, 1844).
11. Danvers Fire Department manuscript records, "Reports of Firewards," Feb. 28, 1850.
12. Tapley, Harriet Silvester, *Chronicles of Danvers*, (Danvers, Danvers Historical Society, 1923), p. 106.
13. Invoice, E. S. Lesley to Town of Danvers, March 26, 1850; Receipt, L. Button & Co. to Danvers Fire Department, Dec. 19, 1854.
14. *Danvers Courier*, Sept. 18, 1847, p. 2, col. 1.
15. *Ibid.*, July 19, 1845, p. 2, col. 2.
16. Danvers Fire Department manuscript records, "Petitions to the Board of Selectmen," Feb. 11, 1830.
17. Danvers Fire Department manuscript records, "Report of committee on Fire Engine," March 29, 1830.
18. "Engine book for fire engine no. 1, Danvers, 1801–1830," *Danvers Historical Society Collections*, v. 32, p. 89–91.
19. *Engine Company No. 6 Record Book*, August, 1850.
20. *Regulations for the Danvers Fire Department*, (Danvers, 1848), p. 6.
21. *Ibid.*, p. 4.
22. Danvers Fire Department manuscript records, *Record Book of Engine No. 2*, September 5, 1835; South Congregational Church reward notice, Oct. 9, 1813 (OR SC R4).
23. *Regulations for the Danvers Fire Department*, (Danvers, 1849), p. 7.
24. Danvers Fire Department manuscript records, *Engine Company No. 6 record book*, March 8, 1845.
25. *Ibid.*, July 10, 1850.
26. Zollo, Richard P. "Danvers Square—An Informal History," *Danvers Historical Society Collections*, v. 43, p. 46.
27. *Engine Company No. 6 Record Book*, March 11, 1856.
28. Wells, John A., *The Peabody Story*, (Salem, Mass., Essex Institute, 1972), p. 334–336.
29. *Salem Observer*, June 14, 1845, p. 2, col. 5.
30. *Ibid.*
31. "Danvers Fires and Fire Companies," *Danvers Historical Society Collections*, v. 5, p. 85.
32. *Danvers Courier*, June 14, 1845, p. 2.
33. *Engine Company No. 6 Record Book*, June 12, 1845.
34. Trask, Richard B., "Historical Commission Building Survey Report No. 371," 1981, p. 1–3.
35. *Engine Company No. 6 Record Book*, October 1, 1856.
36. *Ibid.*, October 9, 1856.
37. "Engine Book for Fire Engine No. 1, Danvers 1801–1830," *Danvers Historical Society Collections*, v. 32, p. 89.
38. *Engine Company No. 6 Record Book*, November 24, 1848.
39. Kirwan, Thomas, *Memorial History of the Seventeenth Regiment*, (Salem, Salem Press, 1911), p. 24–25.
40. *Engine Company No. 6 Record Book*, Aug. 6, 1849.
41. *Ibid.*, Aug. 15, 1849.
42. Danvers Fire Department manuscript records, "Board of Fireward Records," June 8, 1848.
43. *Report of the Committee Chosen to Adjust the Division of Town Property*, (Salem, William Ives, 1857), p. [12] - 13; *Town Meeting Record Book*, v. 11, p. 522–524.
44. Hurd, op. cit., p. 500
45. *Town Meeting Record Book*, v. 11, p. 322–23, 327, 329–330, 472–473, 477.
46. Hurd, op. cit., p. 500–501.

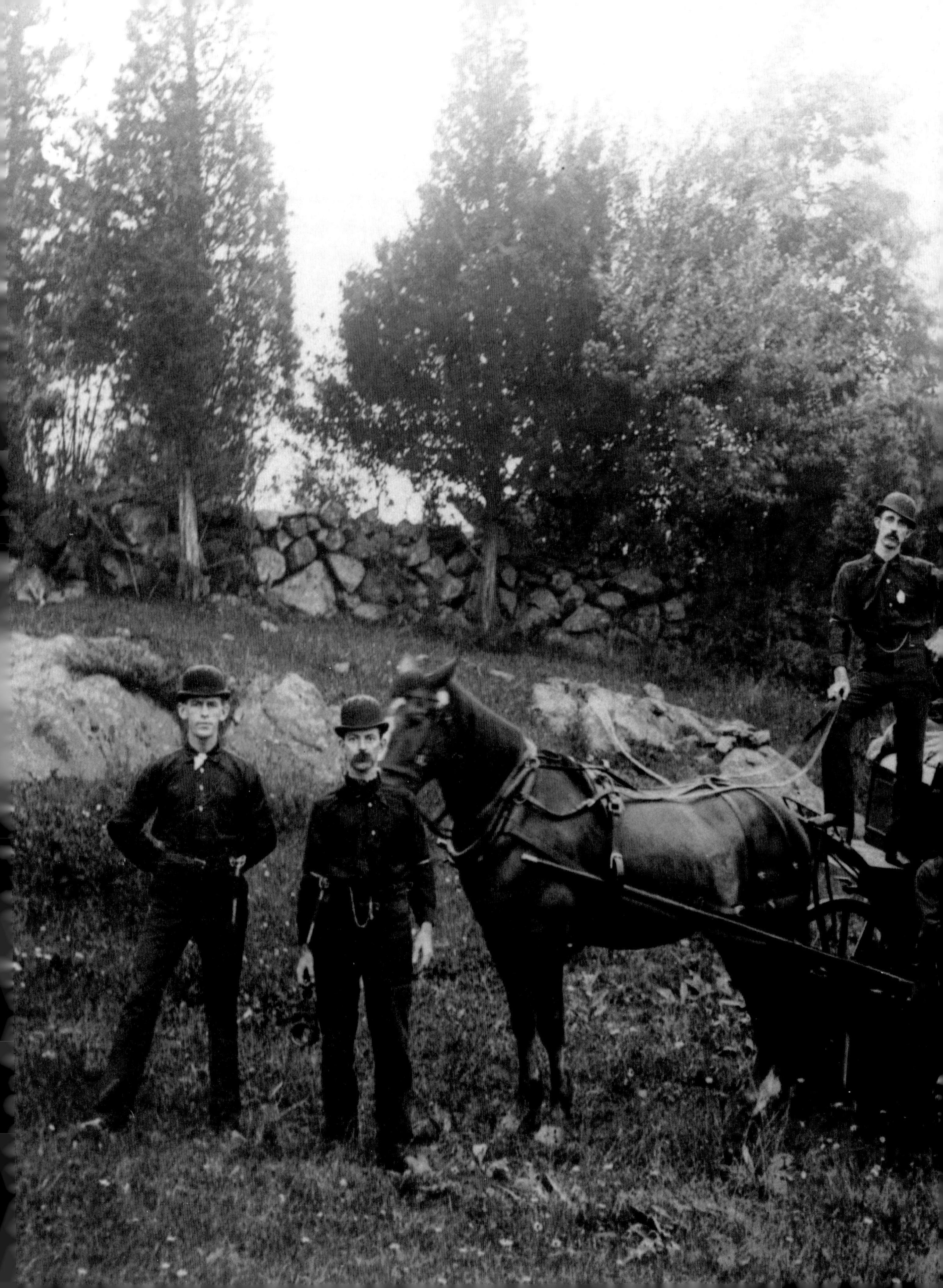

A ca. 1890 photo of one of the Danvers Fire Department hose wagons. Two of the derby hatted men hold the brass pipe (nozzle), while several others wear spanner wrenches on their belts.

Posing in full dress uniform, Ben Chase holds the reins of the hook & ladder truck. Sitting on the ladders in this ca. 1908 photo are from left Harvey E. White and Herbert E. Morrison, while standing on the running board are firemen James Yates, Albert W. Blodgett and Warren Pennell. On the ground are from left Charles Tibbetts, James MacDonald, Jacob B. Pitman, Herbert C. Ham and William Berry.

CHAPTER I

Reorganization Under Chief Kelley

The introduction of the Danvers water system in 1877 had a profound effect upon the fire department. Water pressure from the two hundred new hydrants strategically located around town eliminated the need for man-powered engines. The number of volunteers for each company, like the brakemen who were the pumpers, was drastically reduced. Now only hose companies were necessary with just enough men to connect the hose to the hydrant and direct the pipe or nozzle. The competitiveness of the old volunteer engine companies was over. As the century turned, the cooperative efforts of municipally-employed firefighters took its place.

A listing of the department in 1890 showed the names and locations of the hose companies:

Hose Companies

General Putnam Hose Co. No. 1, School Street.
General Scott Hose Co. No. 2, Holten near Fletcher Street.
Ocean Hose Co. No. 3, River Street.
Major Chase Hose Co. No. 4, School Street.
Hose Co. No. 5, Centre Street.
Hose Co. No. 6, Forest Street.
Hose Co. No. 7, Locust Street.
Matthew Hooper Hose Co. No. 8, Water Street.
Deluge Hose Co. No. 9, Sylvan, opp. Pine Street.

Though several of the companies retained the names of their predecessors, the new rolling equipment was comprised of five hose wagons and four hose reels. Several pungs or low box sleighs holding hose lines were used during the snowy season. Besides a small complement of men, each unit had a foreman and a clerk elected annually.

A new hook and ladder vehicle was purchased in 1892 at a cost of $1,400. It housed a variety of equipment including eight ladders from ten to forty-six feet long, two roof ladders, two six-gallon Babcock extinguishers, axes, bars, shovels, rakes, hooks, and chains. Rubber coats, later called Globe coats after the manufacturer, and hard leather helmets were also given storage area aboard this horse-drawn vehicle.

Though there were a number of smaller fire stations scattered around town, as listed, the former 1839 brick schoolhouse on School Street was taken over by the police and the fire departments. Half of the building was used for Hose Companies 1 and 4 and became known as the Central Fire Station. The hook and ladder truck was housed a short distance away on Maple Street beside the elementary school. In 1895 the town purchased an electric fire alarm system that by 1900 included thirty alarm boxes and several steam whistles connected to the department.

There were shortcomings associated with the hook and ladder set up. In the department's annual report for 1897, Chief Berry noted them:

> We find that the place where the horses are kept now is a long distance from the (hook and ladder) house, being off School Street back of Charles McTernen's harness shop, and when an alarm of fire is sounded, it is more than the driver can do to take both horses at a time to the truck house, having one of them getting away from him on different occasions when it has been attempted. The crowd which is mainly children persists in collecting around the truck house doors, making the horses more excited and difficult to get into the building. After getting them inside, another great difficulty is turning them around to get them along side of the pole, the house being so narrow and cramped for room, so a great deal of valuable time is lost before the piece of apparatus is ready to start. There have been almost five years of experience of this way of working, so we know whereof we speak.

There is a familiar saying, "What goes around, comes around." Today when steps are being taken to reduce the expense of government, it's interesting to discover that in 1899 there was a strong and persistent movement within town government to consolidate the fire, police, and electric light departments with a view toward increasing their efficiency while at the same time reducing the cost of maintenance.

The assertion was made that one chief officer and two assistants, together with a selected force of firemen, from whom four would also act as electrical linemen and special police, could more cheaply do the work of the three existing departments. The fire personnel then consisted of Chief Engineer William A. Berry, four firewards (George Battye, Jay Allard, Joseph Whittier, and Michael Barry), and a number of call men.

In 1908, Ben Chase was taken on to drive the *General Putnam* Hose Company; Elden Swindell, to drive the *General Scott*; and Dan Doyle, to drive *Ocean*.

Town meeting in 1910 voted to appropriate the sum of $2,000 for the purchase of a motorized chemical and hose wagon to replace hose wagon 4. It was also decided to buy a transmitter to be set up in the police station side of the building so that the officer on duty could issue an alarm for any location in Danvers.

Members of Combination 1 pose proudly in front of the Peabody Institute Library. At left is Clarence Shackley and Assistant Chief William Berry, while driver George "Stub" Jones and Aaron Tufts sit in the front seat.

Communications equipment remained in the police station until September of 1926 when the new Central Fire Station at the junction of Maple and Locust Streets was occupied. It stayed there until May 23, 1985, when it and all of our other fire alarm and radio equipment were relocated to the Fire Alarm Dispatch Center at the police station on Ash Street.

On November 4, 1911, the new motorized chemical and hose wagon, the first in Essex County, was put into service. It had been constructed by the Knox Automobile Company of Springfield, Massachusetts, and became our Combination 1. At the same time, George E. Jones, Sr. was hired as a permanent firefighter. Combination 1 remained in faithful service until August 23, 1936. This kit had two thirty-five gallon chemical tanks located under the front seats with the hosebody where the lines or hoses are stored behind. It was started by hand cranking, was chain driven, and had solid rubber tires.

When a call was received on the afternoon of June 25, 1914, at 3:15 from the Salem Fire Department requesting assistance to combat the "Great Salem Fire," Danvers sent Combination 1. Chief Berry was in command. He was aided by Assistant Chiefs Barry and Dennett. George Jones, the driver, was accompanied by eight call men. George Wilson, who was working at the A. C. Lawrence Leather Company on Crowninshield Street in Peabody, left his work and responded on foot. The Danvers Electric Light conveyance made several trips with men, acids, and other supplies.

In all about fifty men went from Danvers. They took up their first position on Cedar near Cherry Street, moved onto Lafayette, where they connected into Engine 27 of Boston with whose crew they stayed throughout the fire. When the pressure in the Salem mains decreased because of the great demand from so many engines, Danvers water was turned into the Salem system at about 3:30 p.m. The local gauge quickly dropped from eighty-four to sixty-eight pounds. Almost simultaneously the Salem gauge increased from twenty-one to sixty-eight pounds. The weary firefighters did not return home until 4:40 a.m. on June 26.

In 1916 the fire department bought its second piece of motorized apparatus. It was a new Ahrens-Fox double piston, eight hundred gallons per minute (g.p.m.) pump, manufactured in Cincinnati, Ohio, and referred to as Engine 1. It was also housed on School Street.

Having bought motorized apparatus and a modern transmitting system, the annual town meeting of 1923 voted to appropriate the sum of $135,000 to build a new central fire headquarters and also acquire a new hook and ladder for the Plains section. Other equipment purchased then included a new combination pump and chemical vehicle to be stationed on High Street in the new Engine 3 fire house, and a new pump for Engine 2 in Tapleyville. It was also passed by a vote of 136-14 that the pay for chauffeurs and relief drivers be increased to $5.00 per day. Article 46 of the agenda set up a committee of citizens to study the needs of the fire department. It was also approved.

In 1924, Danvers hired architect Lester Couch, a native son, to remodel Samuel W. Spaulding's 1859 three and a half story structure for use as the new Central Fire Station. Spaulding, who was a Mason, used his first floor for a store. The third floor was to have been a Masonic Temple with a large hall, but the local Lodge chose to meet elsewhere, so the top two and a half stories

Above: A ca. 1912 photograph displays Danvers' new motorized Knox Combination engine parked at the side of the brick School Street Fire Station.

The 1916 Ahrens-Fox Engine 1 parked in front of the School Street Station. The brick building was originally built as a school house in 1839. By 1900 the building housed two hose companies and the Danvers Police Station.

became a shoe manufactory. In 1918, the Kelmar Shoe Co., Inc., Thomas Kelley, president and treasurer, commenced work here taking over the entire building and employing more than fifty people. The Kelleys' first floor was devoted to a packing and making room; the second, to stitching and cutting rooms; and the third, to storage.

The fire department in 1925 was for the first time fully mechanized and took residence in its new Central Fire Station. According to Town Archivist Richard B. Trask, the former factory had undergone many changes—the construction of a three and a half story bay on the west side, the addition of a hose tower to the rear in which wet lines could be hung up to dry, Palladian-style windows, and a brick veneer facade.

Those town meetings of 1923–1924 were milestone years for the Danvers Fire Department. The special committee that had been appointed in 1923 was charged with the reorganization of the department. Most importantly it was to find a professionally trained fire chief. Engineers Dennett and Barry, along with three other citizens, interviewed fire officers from other municipal departments. Finally on the evening of April 27, 1925, on their recommendation, the Board of Selectmen appointed Joseph E. Kelley, Sr. of Charlestown, the first permanent chief of the Danvers Fire Department.

Born on September 24, 1892, Kelley had been named to the Boston Fire Department in August of 1915. He was a licensed steam engineer for that department and at the time he was called here, he was a captain assigned to its Engine 33. When he received his appointment in Danvers, Dennett and Barry became his assistant engineers. The selectmen that night notified the clerk to send a letter to hose companies 5, 6, 7, 8, and 9 to disband at midnight April 30, 1925, and turn in their badges.

On May 21, 1925, Chief Kelley gave a talk to the Danvers Rotary Club outlining the results of his investigation of the department during the sixteen days he had been here, the released firefighters having been rehired in the meantime. He suggested that the town accept certain legislation to upgrade the fire alarm system and that all members of the department undergo a regular schedule of drills. The Chief told the Rotarians, "The recommendations to the local fire committee and of the insurance exchange (which set the local insurance rates) will be used as a guide to improve the department."

During this transition period, as we have seen, the town had acquired new pieces of motorized apparatus. Most were manufactured by Ahrens-Fox, then the nation's oldest and most prestigious fire engine manufacturer. At the same time the Central Fire Station was being made over, a new Engine 3 fire house, as previously mentioned, had been constructed at the corner of High and Florence Streets. At Engine 2 on Holten Street, the horse stalls were removed and a new heating system and a cement floor were added.

On September 15, 1925, at 4:30 p.m., the Knox Combination 4, driven by Herbert Ham, moved into the Central Fire Station. At 6:45 p.m. Engine 1, driven by George Jones, also reported there. On September 19, our new Ladder 1 was also put into commission at 11:00 a.m. at headquarters. Clarence Amnott was the driver. On September, at 4:00 p.m. a new Engine 2, an $8,000 pump, was in service on Holten Street. Edwin T. Hartman was the driver.   On Saturday, December 19, at 7:20 a.m. Engine 3, which cost $12,500, was placed

A photo of the 1859 Spaulding Building as it looked around 1900, prior to its conversion into the new Central Fire Station.

The 1924 architect's rendering of the remodeling of the Spaulding Building into the new Central Fire Station included three front bay doors and ahose drying tower attached to the rear.

Danvers Fire Chief Joseph Edward Kelley, Sr., who served the town from 1925 to 1958, poses in his uniform near the beginning of his career.

Ladder 1 in front of the new Central Fire Station. Clarence H. Amnott sits in the driver's seat, while standing from left to right are Chief Joseph E. Kelley and firemen Herbert C. Ham, Edwin T. Hartman, George E. Jones, Sr. and William B. Pearson.

The Engine 3 fire house at 130 High Street was built in 1924 in a colonial revival design. The new Ahrens-Fox combination pump and chemical engine (seen in the right bay) was stationed here.

in service on High Street. Francis Regan was the driver. Official work for the fully mechanized Central Fire Station began on September 26, at 9:55 a.m. when Box 24 rang in with what turned out to be a false alarm.

These new engines brought to an end the era of horse-drawn hose wagons and reels. The *General Scott*, *Ocean*, and old Ladder No. 1 were withdrawn from service and the horses released to the street department. It had been an illustrious period in our history.

During Danvers' one hundred fiftieth anniversary celebration in 1902 members of **Ocean Hose Company 3** *pose with their decorated wagon in front of 24 Maple Street.*

Engine 2 was an Ahrens-Fox vehicle put into service in September 1925 and stationed at Holten Street in Tapleyville. Photographed here at the Central Fire Station, Driver Edwin Hartman and Clarence Amnott pose for the camera.

CHAPTER II

Wartime Activities

Under some conditions and situations it may be difficult to believe that there is a standard that fire departments as a whole are governed by. But there are. These standards are dictated by the New England Fire Insurance Rating Association, an organization financially supported by the insurance companies doing business in the region. The Association employs experts like hydraulic, structural, and traffic engineers and building inspectors, all of whom have surveyed Danvers on three different years—1927, 1936, and 1966. These people spend approximately seven days studying the fire defenses of the community, making various recommendations for improvements, and then giving the town or city a grade that its fire insurance rate is based on.

A portion of the Association's 1927 report reveals just how well Danvers had done in a very few years to modernize:

> FIRE DEPARTMENT: Paid. One chief, two assistants and 12 permanent men. 38 call partly paid. Three fire stations. 500 feet of 3" hose. 6,000 feet of 2 1/2" hose. CENTRAL STATION: One Ahrens-Fox triple combination pump (capacity 1,000 gallons) chemical and hose auto truck with 100 ft. of 3" hose and 1100 ft. of 2 1/2" hose. One Ahrens-Fox city service ladder truck with 338 ft. of ladders. One Knox combination hose and chemical auto truck with 1100 ft. of 2 1/2" hose. One Ford supply wagon with 750 ft. of 2 1/2" hose. One chief's car. ENGINE 2: One Ahrens-Fox triple combination pump chemical and hose auto truck with 1100 ft. of 2 1/2" hose. ENGINE 3: One Ahrens-Fox triple combination pump chemical and hose auto truck with 1100 ft. of 2 1/4" hose.
>
> Three pungs in reserve, one in each station. Gamewell fire alarm system. 50 boxes. Headquarters (for the alarm system) in electric station, a brick building.

The Ahrens-Fox trucks carried their ladders on the sides rather than the top of the vehicle; thus they were able to carry more ladders and give a lower center of gravity thereby producing a more stable ride. The pungs were a carry-over from the days of horsepower.

A great asset for Danvers in 1927 had been the work of the Danvers Water Department in laying new mains the previous year. The 12-inch water main between the Square and the State Hospital at Hathorne was replaced by a 20-inch DeLavaud centrifugal, cement-lined cast-iron pipe, Danvers being the first municipality in the East to use this type of pipe.

Two mains had been laid through either side of the Square as far as School Street and then joined into a single 20-inch main that followed the easterly side of Maple Street up to Hathorne. At the State Hospital, the old main going into the reservoir was removed and the new one laid in the same trench.

In this final section, it was necessary to lay the pipe forty-five feet below the surface. This was accomplished by means of a tunnel. The pipe was then encased in concrete for a distance of ninety feet from the reservoir wall out. The work was done by Antonio Mogavero of Peabody.

The reservoir at the State Hospital held five million gallons. A second reservoir in Middleton had a capacity of one and one half million gallons. The benefit to the fire department was that the amount of water pumped into Danvers had been doubled and the number of hydrants raised to three hundred fifty-nine. Under the ground, the town had sixty-three miles of water pipe, 4" to 20" in diameter. The average daily consumption of water here was 1,635,723 gallons.

The reorganization of the fire department continued. After its major reorganization in 1925, refinements were still worked on. The permanent men were working one hundred twenty hours per week and had one day off in five. Bert Ham, George Jones, Sr., William Coleman, and Hollis Skinner were at headquarters. At Engine 2 in Tapleyville were Edwin Hartman and Clarence Clement. Frank Regan and Fred Blodgett were at Engine 3 in Danversport. William A. Berry, an assistant chief, was at the Plains headquarters, and Clarence Dennett, the other, at the 'Port. Not all these people, of course, were on duty at the same time, as some worked the day off for the others. Then on June 1, 1929, the department went into what is commonly referred to as a two-platoon system, and the workload for the men was reduced from one hundred twenty hours to eighty-four. John D. Madison was appointed a permanent firefighter at this time.

Firefighter John D. Madison joined the Danvers force in 1928. He retired in 1960 and was described by Chief Martin as one of the best firefighters he ever knew. Madison died in 1976.

At the town meeting of March 22, 1926, the voters were asked to accept the provision of Chapter Nine of the General Laws of the Act of 1926 placing the office of the chief engineer of the Danvers Fire Department under civil service. The words "chief engineer" meant chief of the department. The vote was Yes, 1,582; No, 1,239. However, during the same meeting, Article Fifty-Nine asked the voters to place the permanent firefighters also under civil service at the petition of Ralph E. Pitman and others. Action on this article was indefinitely postponed. It wasn't until some years later that the men came under civil service.

In his annual report in 1926, Chief Kelley stated that the department had responded to two hundred sixty-five calls and that all buildings and apparatus were in excellent condition. As a result of the work on the water mains, nine new fire alarm boxes had been added to the system, and the system itself was retimed to two seconds for a faster response. The Chief also reported that the reciprocal assistance arrangement made the year before between Peabody, Beverly, and

A Pierce Arrow truck was converted by George E. "Stub" Jones, Sr. into this the fire department's foam truck.

Danvers had proven successful. The Chief then received a salary of $2,000 per year; the seven permanent men each got $1,825.

A great source of pride to the regular firefighters has always been their ability to use skills, often previously learned, for the benefit of the department and thus the town. For example, George E. Jones, Sr. had been a blacksmith before his appointment in 1911. In 1929 "Stub," as he was affectionately called because of his short stature, converted a Pierce Arrow truck into a foam vehicle to fight oil and chemical fires by blanketing and thereby smothering them. It was referred to as Foam Truck 6. It carried a foam-maker, foam, and hose.

My own vivid memories of the department began in the 1930s. On the morning of May 12, 1935, Box 15 was struck at 6:15 a.m. followed a few minutes later by a general alarm. This was the beginning of the end of Batchelder's icehouse. Over the years, ice had been harvested from the Mill Pond in late winter. Then it was carried by way of an elevated ramp over Sylvan Street and into the icehouse with its heavily insulated double walls for storage.

I was only nine years old at the time, but I clearly remember walking with Mrs. Kelley, the chief's wife, and my mother from our house on Chase Street to the grounds of the Peabody Institute Library from which vantage point we watched. This was the first multiple-alarm fire that I can ever recall witnessing.

On August 4, 1936, the Knox Combination, now Engine 4, that had been put into service on November 4, 1911, was replaced by a Pirsch triple combination pumping engine for $5,477. It was manufactured by the Peter Pirsch & Sons Company of Kenosha, Wisconsin. A new chief's car was also acquired, a four-

A 1936 view of Chief Kelley and his car equipped with sirens, lights and special plate on the front.

door 1936 Dodge. During World War II, approximately in 1944, the car needed a new battery, but there were none available as they were rationed. Apparently our chief was not very high on the priority list for a new one. I can remember many a night during two winters pushing the car out of the chief's garage at 20 Bayview Avenue. The sloping driveway was just sufficient to start it.

Near the beginning of World War II, the American automobile industry no longer produced civilian vehicles, so the Danvers Fire Department began the practice of buying secondhand trucks for conversion. In 1940, for instance, a used 1936 one-ton Chevrolet truck was made over into an apparatus used primarily for woods and grass fires. It was fitted with a five hundred gallon, front-mounted pump and a four hundred ten gallon booster tank, the latter supplying the small lines, by Phillip A. Wood Co., a small apparatus manufacturer in Topsfield. It was referred to as Engine 7.

In the same year, a 1937 half-ton Dodge pickup became Engine 6. Equipped with hand-operated pumps that held five gallons of water each and a five hundred g.p.m. midship skid pump, this rig was found to be particularly well adapted for use by the approximately twenty civilian defense firefighters. These men all wore white helmets like a World War I doughboy's but with a Maltese cross on the front. In order to put out possible fires started by an enemy bombing raid

During World War II the vehicles at Central Fire Station included the 1916 Ahrens-Fox Engine 1 (at right), the 1936 Pirsch Engine 4 (second from left) and late 1930s second-hand Chevrolet truck (at left) made into Engine 7. A Dodge pickup (second from right) was converted into Engine 6.

(such was the power on the imagination of the newsreel shots of the Blitz over London), they placed containers of sand on board also.

In 1940 the Central Fire Station's first and second floor meeting rooms were fitted with wooden blackout panels so that during raids the lights within the station could remain on. The air raid communication center was located in a partitioned off section of the second floor. It had one large table, approximately five feet wide and fifteen feet in length, on which were nearly a dozen telephones. This room was manned twenty-four hours a day by a paid civilian warden. (There were many officers in the Civil Defense Corps by very few privates.)

Among this warden's duties the principal one was to make hourly checks by phone to area headquarters, wherever that was, and in the event of enemy attack, he would be the first one in town to be informed. He would then notify the person in charge of the fire department who, in turn, would transmit the air raid warning over the audible fire alarm system. Responding to this warning, designated representatives from various town offices, the Red Cross, and the chief air warden of the town would assemble at the Central Fire Station. The warden would position himself at the head of the table and be in overall command of the situation.

Along with the adults, there would be several Boy Scouts who were to act as messengers during these drills. They would be dispatched to different parts of the town with urgent messages. Being a member of Troop No. 1, Boy Scouts of America, I was one of those messengers. I pedaled miles throughout Danvers on my bicycle during many practice attacks.

When war came, local firefighters were either very young or middle-aged fellows too old to serve in the armed forces. Looking back on this period, I must say that it was the height of volunteerism. Everybody wanted to play a role.

The Maple Street Church steeple is fully ablaze and ready to topple in this May 20, 1944, photo.

CHAPTER III

The 1850 Maple Street Church Leveled

The material for the period covered in this book up through about 1944, I gathered by talking and working with firefighters and others who experienced the events firsthand and then related the facts to me. For the years between 1944 and the present time, 1991, most of the incidents recalled I personally participated in or was a witness thereof.

Off Endicott Street behind the plant now known as Devcon Corp., there was an historic century-old railroad bridge over Waters River. On a blustery cold March afternoon in 1943 as the 2:00 p.m. train was crossing over the one hundred ninety-four foot span, hot coals apparently fell from the steam engine onto the heavily creosoted ties. Shortly thereafter a call was received from Creese and Cook's at 33 Water Street that the bridge was on fire.

Engine 3 was the only company available to respond as all of the other apparatus were out to grass and brush fires. The fire rapidly engulfed the structure so that there was no stopping the flames. The nearest hydrant was located out on Endicott Street. It took nearly two thousand feet of line to deliver water onto the fire. Peabody assisted by attacking the fire from the other side, but the men there also had a great distance to lay their hose. Within a short time, the railroad tracks were twisted and bent out of shape. It was nearly a year before the Boston & Maine trains could pass over the river again.

In the early 1950s, the bridge caught fire again with the same result. Then history repeated itself a third time in 1971 when youngsters lit a grass fire that ignited the nearby bridge. However, the result was not so disastrous as it had been for the previous two fires. Although the bridge could not be used again until extensive repairs were made, it was not a total loss. A contributing factor in dousing the flames so swiftly was the use of a floating pump that drew water from the river. It had been purchased by the department on the strong recommendation of Deputy Chief Richard Wessell.

Nineteen forty-four was the middle of the war and most of our young, energetic call men were in the armed forces. Gardner Trask had been sent to Greenland; Joe Kelley, Jr. was in North Africa; Webby Dwinell, in New Caledonia; and Joe Farley of Twilight League fame and my predecessor as chief of the department was in the Air Force as an airplane mechanic. There were others serving as well.

Devastation within the Maple Street Church sanctuary.

On the warm evening of Saturday, May 20, at 9:45 p.m., George Jones, Jr. was looking out the station doors at fire headquarters when he observed flames reflected in the windows of the Maple Street School. He immediately opened the apparatus doors and pulled Box 12. Engine 4 and Ladder 1 responded from there. The engine went down the driveway to the Maple Street Congregational Church carriage shed, a long one-story structure with about a half dozen open bays. Here in earlier days carriages would be parked while the owners and their families attended services. The shed was burning fiercely.

When Engine 4 pulled in front of this shed, Frank Finnegan knew right away that they could not control the fire with the small amount of water—eighty gallons—in the booster tank. He then did the only prudent thing; he backed his kit out of the driveway and threw the hose rope around the hydrant in front of the church and laid the line down the driveway to the structure.

By this time the chief and several call men had arrived. Since the shed was old and in disrepair, the fire was making considerable headway, so the chief ordered Engine 3 which had just arrived from its High Street station, to lay another line from in front of the school and come into the carriage shed with it.

Keep in mind now that there were no radios then; thus all orders had to be given by a hearty yell.

As the men were laying the second line, call firefighter Charles Nimblett of Engine 3 peering through the narrow strips of windows on either side of the back door, saw flames inside the rear hallway of the church. The men then forced their way in through this door and advanced up a short flight of stairs into a corridor that ran from one side of the church to the other. After going a little farther, they realized that there was fire beneath them and that the partitions to their right, directly behind the altar, were very hot and charged with flame. The chief immediately had Jack Madison return to headquarters to transmit a general alarm to summon help from Salem, Peabody, Beverly, Topsfield, and Middleton.

This edifice was nearly one hundred years old and built of heavy timber construction. (See "Looking Back," p. 30–31.)

This second fire had started in the basement in an area between the two lower halls, one located at the front of the church and one at the rear. The fire spread rapidly from this point into the partition behind the altar and extended up into the cockloft or small attic of the main church. There were no fire stops so that the fire had clear passage. Flames and heated gases were drawn up into the steeple producing a chimney effect.

The timbers of the rear side of the spire were most severely engulfed in flame and weakened first, causing it to fall back into the church. It is a myth to think that church steeples are built to fall back this way into the church during fires. The rear timbers and support of the steeple are the first ones to be affected by the flames and collapse, thereby causing the spire to fall backward.

At this time, I was very young but very much interested in the Danvers Fire Department. Gardner Trask had loaned me, while he was off in the United States Navy, a night hitch, an outfit that consisted of heavy trousers with suspenders and a pair of boots that were much too large for me. With the boots tucked inside the trousers (later coveralls), a fireman places the hitch beside his cot at night so that it can be put on in seconds when an alarm comes in.

The evening of the fire, I had gone down to the Paramont Theatre in Salem. As my bus was passing through Gardner Park, I could see the glow from the fire. I got off the bus at the end of Bayview Avenue and ran up the hill to my house where I quickly changed my clothes and then rode my bicycle to the fire scene.

Shortly after my arrival, I came across Chief Kelley; Father Michael F. Collins, a spark from Marblehead who became Chaplain of the New England Association of Fire Chiefs; Leo Nimblett, who was a call man and superintendent of the Danvers Electric Light Department; and Carlton M. Stearns, a deacon of the church. They were discussing the possibility of entering the structure and rescuing the communion service. I asked if I might join them and much to my gleeful surprise, I was not told that I could not, so I went in too and proceeded down the same hallway to a closet where the vessels were kept. There Mr. Stearns handed me all the trays of goblets that I could carry. Along with the others, I made my exit down the smoke-filled hall and back out into the fresh air.

Raymond J. Guppy, a dedicated call firefighter who subsequently became a permanent and loyal member of our department, had spent the weekend in Boxford. He was also a long standing member of the congregation and sang in the choir. Returning to Danvers the following morning to attend services, he dis-

The exterior of the church as revealed Sunday morning. The congregation's vitality of spirit is noted by a sign posted on a front pillar reading, "Service Today 11 a.m. Masonic Temple."

covered the devastation. Searching through the rubble that morning, Raymond found the bell, which had a diameter of five feet.

On June 1, 1944, while Ladder 1 was responding to Box 31, the rear cylinder box cracked rendering it inoperable. After the vehicle had been examined by a mechanic from Lord & Herlihy's garage at 154 Maple Street, it was found that the engine could not be repaired. This vehicle was only eighteen years old. The chief then made arrangements to borrow another Ahrens-Fox City Service ladder truck from Cambridge. It was in service until November of 1947 when our new sixty-five foot Pirsch aerial ladder arrived.

At the annual town meeting on March 4, 1945, Article Eight, stipulating that a committee of three be designated to make a survey of the manpower needs of the fire department and present it at the next town meeting, was passed unanimously. The three members chosen for the manpower committee were Theodore A. Bean, Philip H. Couhig, and Joseph Caliga. They did an in-depth study of the situation and all agreed that the department was definitely undermanned. In fact, its personnel had remained the same since the reorganization in 1925. Many comparisons were done between our department and those of surrounding communities. Their abridged recommendations in 1946 were as follows:

The 1947 Pirsch aerial ladder in service during a fire at 140 High Street in about 1964. This early house had to be demolished as a result of the fire. At left is Engine 4 acquired by the town in 1962.

1. The department be increased to sixteen permanent men and twenty-three call men.
2. Beginning March 1, 1947, no call men should be over sixty-five.
3. Beginning March 1, 1946, no new call men should be appointed who worked out of Danvers during the day.
4. Specific training sessions be scheduled and carried out.
5. The office of assistant fire engineers be abolished as of 1946.
6. The department be governed by the chief of the department.
7. As soon after the war as possible two-way radio equipment be installed.

Also at this town meeting, the chief submitted a budget of $63,722.16. The major increases were for a 10 percent increase in pay for all permanent men, the addition of six permanent men commencing June 3, and the purchase of a new aerial ladder truck for $16,500. This piece of apparatus was put into service on November 12, 1947, and Charles Doyle drove it on its first run, a false alarm at Maple and Forest Streets.

Our next new apparatus, which came three years later on October 30, 1948, would be radically different from all our previous engines. It was a new one thousand g.p.m. American LaFrance pump, designated Engine 1. The cost was

The 1948 American LaFrance Engine 1 in action in September 1962. Ray Guppy uses the deck gun to begin knocking down a fire at the Danvers State Hospital barns.

$15,500. Powered by the company's famous V-12 engine, its innovative design placed the cab in front of both the engine and the front axle, thereby giving better forward vision to the driver. Compact and with a short turning radius, this cab-ahead model was more maneuverable around corners. Three men could ride on the front seat and two more behind them on jumpseats on either side of the engine. There was space for an additional three men on the rear step. It came equipped with a Motorola ten-watt radio, making it the first Danvers Fire Department vehicle with a radio. Its base station was located at headquarters. In 1948, the chief's car was also given a two-way radio. Our frequency was 46.12, and our call letters were KCI243.

On June 19, 1945, Firefighter John (Dud) Lynch, who was alone at Engine 2, was found dead by Chief Kelley when he did not respond to the 6:45 a.m. test.

Appointed in 1929, the forty-five year old Lynch had been on duty at a station where there was only one man on duty at a time.

The year 1946 saw the beginning of the end of an era. Many of our first permanent men—Jones, Ham, and some of those appointed in 1925 during the reorganization—were retiring and the new blood, the young blood, now joined our department. Phil Davis, Charlie Doyle, Joe Kelley, Jr., Joe Kinsella, Webby Dwinell, Joe Farley, John M. Noonan, and Ronald Sturtevant, all joined the force on June 1, 1946. Ray Guppy came in on December 5, 1946. Many of them had been call men previous to entering the military. Several, like Phil Davis, brought back the experience and training they had received in the armed forces.

After returning home from my own tour of duty with the U.S. Navy in the South Pacific, I went back to Holten High School and got my diploma. In early July 1946, while I was paying my parents' electric light bill, Leo Nimblett asked me if I wanted to "run" for him. What that meant was that when a box alarm was transmitted and later when the apparatus had returned to quarters, a roll call was taken, and Leo would be given credit for my attendance. He then signed his call-man's check over to me.

On weekends and at various other times, I would sleep in at headquarters. I shared the room with Davis, who subsequently became the first captain of the Danvers Fire Department under civil service. I can recall being so eager that I could hardly fall asleep in anticipation of the bell striking and the night lights coming on. I saw myself throwing the bedclothes off, donning my sweat shirt and my night hitch, sliding down the pole to the apparatus floor, and then putting on my rubber coat and helmet. The captain would open the doors, and we would roar out to our next adventure. What a thrill to a teenage kid! How I loved it. I still do. So when Leo asked me that day to run for him another dream had been fulfilled. I substituted for him from then to the date of my appointment. Leo was a true friend, and I will always be grateful to him.

A leather helmet used into the 1950s by Danvers Call Fireman Gardner S. Trask.

Nineteen forty-seven brought several changes to the department, both in manpower and equipment. Firefighting supplies were becoming available with, as noted, modern innovations learned in the military. One of the principal ones was the technique of using water in the form of minute droplets. This was commonly referred to as a fog pattern. Lloyd Layman, a U.S. Navy firefighter, developed this technique for combatting shipboard fires. At that time, the Danvers Fire Department also purchased the first of its self-contained breathing equipment.

67

An aerial view on Maple Street showing the Fossa Block fire of February 17, 1950.

CHAPTER IV

Adventures of a Young Danvers Firefighter

At the annual town meeting in March of 1947, it was voted to increase the department's personnel by four firemen, thus bringing the total complement to eighteen, and to reduce the working hours from eighty-four to seventy-two hours per week.

A firefighter's examination was scheduled for June 2. Under civil service rules, I was ineligible, for I had not reached the age of twenty-one. Through the help of Chief Kelley and his good friend Everett Bacheller, our town's representative to the General Court, an act was presented to the House amending Chapter Thirty-One by inserting the following section, 22A: "Any veteran who will have attained the age of twenty-one within six months of the date of a scheduled examination for police or fire services shall not be deemed ineligible for examination and appointment because of the established minimum age requirement to take such exam." The bill passed in the Senate on April 10 and in the House on April 21.

On June 29, 1947, four new men were named to the Danvers Fire Department: Melvin King, James Horgan, William Murphy, and Leland E. Martin.

I was stationed at headquarters, and Francis Regan became my captain. My first tour of duty was Monday, June 30, at 8:00 a.m. John Noonan was then the driver of Engine 4 and Charles Doyle, of the Cambridge ladder truck. My post was on the rear step of Engine 4. My first response was a still alarm at 1:35 p.m. It was for a dump fire behind the Friend Box Company at 90 High Street. The first audible box alarm I answered was Box 34 at 7:14 p.m. on July 5 for a grass fire. These initial alarms were very exciting to me, for I was now a real firefighter receiving $35.00 a week and going to fires.

It was a cold January day in 1950. I was at headquarters where we were checking the crosslinks of the tire chains. At about 10:30 a.m. the phone rang. A four-year-old child had fallen through the ice at the Meadow. Engine 1 and Ladder 5 immediately proceeded up Hobart Street, turned down Wadsworth, where there was a cluster of people near Pete's Garage. Captain Madison told Joe Farley to stop Engine 1 there. The ladder truck pulled up behind us.

We went down behind the garage to the edge of the ice. Some neighbors were pointing out over the expanse to the still unfrozen channel. I ran out onto

The old 1925 Ahrens-Fox Engine 3, renumbered "5", at work in front of Wells Drug Store, while the 1947 Pirsch Aerial Ladder reaches to the Fossa Block roof.

the ice and over to the clear water a considerable distance from shore. I looked down into the clear, icy depth, and turning I yelled over my shoulder that I could see a small red jacket. Every one of the men called out, "Dive in!"

I quickly threw off my heavy Globe coat and dove into approximately eight feet of water. I grabbed the youngster's collar and with one tremendous kick, pushed us to the surface. Then I swam over to the edge where Joe and Charlie extended a rake, a long pole with a hook on the end. I put the collar of the jacket over the hook, and they pulled the boy onto safe ice. Joe picked him up and ran toward the waiting Pulmotor and Sullivan's ambulance. Later I learned that the boy had perished.

I had been left alone in all the excitement. Every time I attempted to get onto the ice, it broke away. Once when I tried to lift my leg out of the water, I felt one of my boots slide off. Finally Charlie Doyle returned with the rake and pulled me onto solid ice. I recovered my coat and put it on. With only one boot on, I headed for shore. I returned to headquarters on Engine 1. The chief greeted me, noticed my missing boot, and sent me upstairs to take a shower.

The February 1950 fire at the apartment complex at 32 Holten Street.

John Ellsworth and other members of the highway department on the morning of February 17, 1950, were removing snow from the Square when Ellsworth observed smoke coming out of the Rat Hole, a bowling alley owned by Thomas Kontos in the basement of the Fossa Block. John promptly went across the street and pulled Box 14. Upon his arrival, Chief Kelley ordered a second alarm and subsequently a general alarm summoning aid from several other communities.

At about 8:00 a.m., I was on a line that we had advanced through the front door of Wells Drugstore as far as the area where the prescriptions were kept. Firefighter Charles Kuell and I made several trips removing them. At one point, I re-entered the store and went to the soda fountain where I helped myself to a very generous vanilla ice cream cone. Upon exiting, I nearly ran into Chief Kelley. He made a few uncomplimentary remarks, and the cone and I rapidly parted company.

The fire was finally brought under control about mid–afternoon and overhauling or the search for hidden fires took place well into the night. All the barber chairs in Zollo's Barber Shop ended up in the cellar and had to be removed the following day by a wrecker from Sullivan's Garage. It was one of the most obstinate fires that I have ever encountered. In all, eleven businesses and nine offices were gutted by this very stubborn, smoky fire. The total loss amounted to more than $500,000.

Another notable fire occurred later in February of 1950 at 32 Holten Street about 3:30 a.m. As we pulled up in front of the building, the basement windows were cherry red with flame. Joe Kelley was driving Engine 4, Jack Madison was the captain, and I was on the rear step. Charlie Doyle was driving the ladder truck. I started to dress the hydrant when Captain Madison yelled to me, "Never mind connecting the hose. Let's get in there and get the people out."

He and Joe went into the first floor and assisted people out. I ran up the back stairs and as I did, tongues of flames were lapping out between the risers and treads. I recall vividly that I was very scared. Oh, what a thrilling experience it was! I was all alone, but I was going to save people's lives.

I went into the second floor rear apartment where I found an elderly couple. I assisted the woman onto the aerial ladder which Charlie had thrown to their bedroom window. I then assisted the gentleman down the stairs and safely out. I re-entered the house with Joe Kinsella. We went up to the third floor and again helped people out. Although the fire spread from the cellar and through the roof by way of the partitions and stairshafts, the property was repaired and is still there.

One of the more memorable experiences in my early years happened on March 2, 1951 at 11:45 a.m. I was alone on duty at Engine 3. I can remember very clearly that it was Thursday because all the bright work (brass) had to be polished. I had just completed this task when Box 5 at the corner of Bridge and Elliott Streets hit. I immediately opened the doors and started the engine of the old 1925 seven hundred fifty gallon Ahrens-Fox piston pump. I turned left from High onto Liberty Street. After passing the lumber sheds of Calvin Putnam Lumber Company, I glanced in the direction of the alarm box and saw a pillar of black smoke several hundred feet in the air. I crossed over Spite Bridge. My heart started to pound. I was by myself and my back-up was a good four to five minutes away.

Because of the color of the smoke, I wondered, is it an oil or gasoline truck? Or could it be a small airplane? As I approached the intersection of Elliott and Liberty, I had to stand up, there being no cab on this old vehicle and the chrome-plated pulsation dome obstructed part of my view. Proceeding past the little brick Williams School, I could again see the smoke. Closer to the intersection of Elliott and Bridge Streets, I observed that it was the Bradstreet tenement house at 12 Bridge.

I passed by the nearest hydrant and pulled into the entrance of the driveway, for I first wanted to see if there was anyone remaining in the rambling two and a half story structure. After alighting, I went down the short driveway to the rear door. The entire side of the building was engulfed in flame.

Several people assured me that everyone was out. Knowing there was no life hazard, I then made a quick "size up" of the situation and determined that I

This Ahrens-Fox Engine 3, here with Francis Daniel Regan sitting in front of the High Street station, was the one on which Leland Martin responded to the Bridge Street fire.

    Several people assured me that everyone was out. Knowing there was no life hazard, I then made a quick "size up" of the situation and determined that I needed to lay a line. As I was backing up the pump to the hydrant, I remember thinking, "Oh my God, I'm alone, and I have to dress the hydrant and then lay the line from there to the fire." Connecting the hose and the quarter turn gate valve to control the flow of water in that single line and then laying the hose were jobs for two men.

    At that point, a young man, unknown to me, said, "I'll take care of the hydrant." He knew what he was doing because he took the hose rope and placed it over the hydrant, and then he yelled to me, "Go!" I ran out the line, and as I was attaching the nozzle, Engine 1 arrived. To me, it had seemed like an eternity.

    The fire had begun in the rear hall where a window had broken from the heat. Flames extended not only up the rear stairshaft, but also out through that melted window to the asphalt shingles, the cause of the black smoke, and rapidly engulfed the entire southerly side of the house. Although there was severe fire damage, we left the building virtually intact when we left.

Members of "Danvers Citizen's Hose." Mugging for the camera in fake moustaches and kepi hats are from left, Francis W. "Webbie" Dwinell, Bernard Lyons, Leland Martin, George Wilson, John M. "Mike" Noonan, two unidentified men, Wilfred A. "Fred" Vaillancourt, Joseph M. Kinsella, Lloyd E. Pennell and Raymond J. Guppy. The buckets, two leather hats and fire trumpets are from the 1890 era of the fire department.

CHAPTER V

Firemen's Musters and Forest Fires

The revival of the old firemen's musters around 1951 stirred considerable interest within the fire departments of New England. These contests began in the fierce rivalry between fire clubs of America before 1850. Our revived musters had rules for different kinds of apparatus. They were held in various communities during the warm months on about a bi-monthly basis. With the exception of the Grand Muster held on July Fourth, they were usually conducted on Saturdays.

Festivities began with a parade of the visiting hand tubs and old motorized kits. Many were more than eighty years old. Occasionally an impressive, horse-drawn steamer or two appeared. Following this, there was a collation served at the local park. After a hearty meal and a round of liquid refreshments, the muster would start off with the competitions to determine, for example, which hose company could lay the quickest one hundred fifty feet of hose and have water delivered from the nozzle. Always the main event was a spirited contest to ascertain which apparatus could shoot a stream of water the farthest.

Not to be outdone by our brothers from other towns, several of us Danvers permanent and call men banded together and formed a volunteer unit, the Danvers Citizen's Hose Company. The first vehicle we owned, a 1930 Maxim rotary gear pump, had once been the property of the Citizen's Hose Company of Danbury, Connecticut. From 1940-1951, it had seen service with a volunteer company in York, Maine. We got it from Phillip A. Wood Co., of Topsfield. That firm had taken it as a trade in towards a new pump which Wood built for the York company. He donated the Maxim to our use to attend musters throughout Massachusetts, New Hampshire, and Maine.

There were in all approximately twenty-five members in the Danvers Citizen's Hose Company. Nearly every Saturday we attended a muster. We went as far north as York, Maine, south to the Cape, and west to Fitchburg. We were a hearty band of young and middle-aged firefighters, and we kept the spirit of the old-time firemen's musters alive for more than ten years.

On July 15, 1952, at 10:00 a.m., a mammoth parade starting at Dexter Woodman Square in the 'Port kicked off the bicentennial anniversary of the town of Danvers. The region's firefighters, with eight hundred fifty men, made up the fifth division of this procession. Music for the marching delegations was furnished by the Boston Fire Department Band. Following the marching units came sixteen old hand tubs from the three-state area. There were over fifty pieces of motorized apparatus, as well as hand-drawn and horse-drawn antique kits.

Let me give you an idea of the size of the fire department division. As the head of it passed the reviewing stand in front of the old National Bank at 17 Maple Street, the rear of the division was just turning from High Street onto Elm. Following the line of march on the Plains—Elm Street, Holten Street, Charles Street, Pickering to Hobart, and then down Maple Street, through the Square—those firefighters and their apparatus covered a distance of over a mile.

Leland Martin drives Ladder 5 down High Street accompanied by Gardner S. Trask during Danvers' two hundredth anniversary parade in 1952.

For local people, more exciting than the appearance of the five horse-drawn steamers was that of old *Ocean No. 3* once from Danversport. Later in the day seventeen of the hand pumpers engaged in competitions held at Plains Park. Old *Ocean No. 3*, then known as the *Passaconaway* of Seabrook, New Hampshire, took first honors in Class A.

As late as 1953 there was a strong spirit of rivalry between Danvers call men, especially in Engines 2 and 3. In 1951 Engine 2 had their apparatus replaced with an American LaFrance 1000 g.p.m. pump. The call men from Engine 3 vowed, "We will have nothing less than what Engine 2 has, or better." There was considerable talk then of purchasing a less expensive commercial vehicle for them rather than a custom pump like those at Engines 1 and 2. The

Members of Engine 1 respond at Central Headquarters to a fire in 1953. From left are Firefighters P. Francis Finnegan stepping into the cab, Charles H. Kuell by left rear step, Francis W. Dwinell putting on his coat, and Captain John Joseph Farley coming down the pole.

matter was resolved when the town meeting in 1953 voted to acquire an American LaFrance 1000 g.p.m., two-stage centrifugal pump with a two hundred gallon booster tank, which was delivered in the fall of that year to Engine 3.

Our department's apparatus at this time was second to none on the North Shore. We had three modern state-of-the-art one thousand gallon pumping engines equipped also with 1000 g.p.m. deck guns. Engine 3's new apparatus replaced our 1925 Ahrens-Fox piston pump of seven hundred fifty gallons capacity, and Engine 2 had a foam proportioner, making possible the correct mix of foam and water. We had a sixty-five foot aerial ladder and Engine 7 was used as a brush-fire truck.

Aside from our apparatus, our firefighting equipment was improving with great rapidity. All our nozzles were now standardized with Akron variable-flow fog nozzles, both one and two and a half inch sizes. These devices break the water down into fine droplets to provide a narrow or wide fog pattern. We had sufficient air masks for all members, and all were equipped with aluminum helmets, Globe coats, and safety-toed boots. All vehicles had radios, and Engine 1 had a portable radio. In early 1954, a new chief's car, a Dodge, was put into service to replace the 1946 Oldsmobile.

As to personnel, all groups now had permanent captains. In 1951 Philip W. Davis received his captain's appointment. In 1952 Joseph Farley, Joseph Kelley, Jr., and Ronald Sturtevant received theirs. All companies held daily drills. In-service inspections were commenced, and the overall standard of the department was shaping up to be very progressive and sophisticated.

During the spring and early summer of 1953, there was a severe drought throughout New England. Danvers had several woods fires, especially in the area of the town forest and Pedrick Woods. Southern Maine experienced extensive and drastic forest fires. As a result, on Friday, August 15, that state's forest service sent out a plea for volunteers to help combat the numerous fires.

The Danvers Citizen's Hose Company was activated. We left early the following morning from the Central Fire Station headed for Sanford Airfield. All through that night we labored until we were relieved by a fresh crew and returned home.

On March 8, 1955, the historic 1891 Trask barn in East Danvers beside Route 128 was gutted by fire. At the time it was leased out to a local contractor. One of his employees had been welding a piece of equipment. The hot slag from this operation ignited a pile of debris in a corner of the barn. Shortly thereafter, it caused a raging inferno. When the welder realized the predicament he was in, he got into his pickup truck and drove frantically to the Central Fire Station more than a mile away to alert us. In his haste, he had passed five fire alarm boxes and two telephone construction crews working on Poplar Street. Consequently there was a delay in our response.

Mr. Charles Trask, owner of the barn that had been in his family for generations, was at work at his brokerage firm on State Street in Boston. When he heard of the fire, he immediately returned home in a taxi cab. At this fire, Captain Joseph E. Kelley, Jr., son of Chief Kelley, injured himself quite badly while taking the heavy deck gun down from atop Engine 3. Today the barn has been renovated into a four-story modern office building.

This same year, 1955, the Loyal Order of Moose organized a civilian defense auxiliary fire department. There were untold amounts of surplus government equipment from the Korean War, and it goes without saying that this federally supported spin-off of the department was very well supplied. But as with many strictly volunteer groups, interest did not last long and like with the melting snow in the spring, our auxiliary fire department soon vanished.

We experienced a major change on February 27, 1957. From the reorganization of the department in 1925, there had been only one man stationed at Engines 2 and 3. This was a very unsafe practice, but not uncommon at all within the region's fire services. But the weakness was recognized, especially after the death of Dud Lynch in 1945. A serious incident had occurred when there was a fire in a two-family residence, and the people were endangered in both the first and second floors. The lone firefighter could only attempt one rescue. The others were saved by the next crew to arrive. After that our department increased to a total of twenty-eight permanent members, so that Engines 2 and 3 were each assigned two men.

The Danvers diving team suited up on Porter River. Included are from left, Captain Joseph E. Kelley, Jr., Robert G. Osgood, Chief Joseph E. Kelley, Wilfred A. Vaillancourt, and kneeling from left, Sarafine Perry, Leland Martin, James A. McInnis, and Joseph Santorella. Bob Guerrette, wearing civilian clothes, assisted in this instruction.

In the early spring of 1957, a tragic accident occurred in the pond that used to be located off Summer Street in the vicinity of St. John's Prep. It no longer exists as it was later drained and the area was subdivided into house lots. On a warm spring day two young boys were out on the pond on a raft when one of them fell off and drowned. Shortly thereafter, his parents and a service organization within the town donated sufficient funds to provide for equipping and training several members of the department as a diving team. Its members included Captain Joseph E. Kelley, Jr. and firefighters Sarafine Perry, Jim McInnis, Joseph Santorella, Bob Osgood, Fred Vaillancourt, and me. After extensive training under the expertise of Jim Cahill of Salem, an ex-Navy frogman, our diving team participated in many water-related emergencies. Most notable among these was the rainy, cold night in November 1961 when a large jet aircraft went into Boston Harbor.

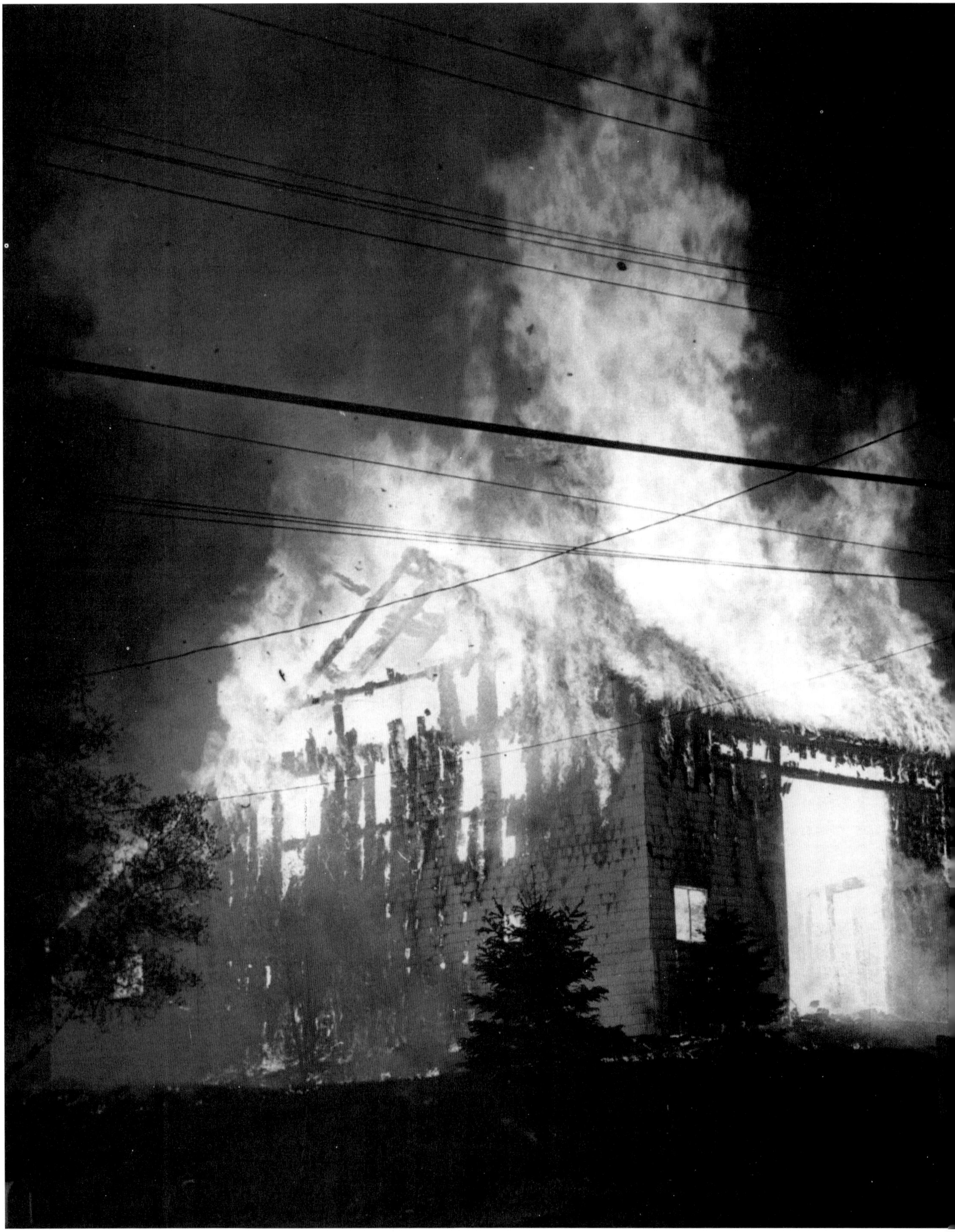

A spectacular barn fire erupted at 381 Andover Street in 1961. Though the ca. 1838 William Goodale house also caught on fire, the fire department was able to save the historic structure.

Posing for this June 1953 photo on Engine 3 is driver James Horgan, while below from left are Firefighters Raymond Guppy, George LaChance, Sylvio Morin, Francis Talbot, Bernard Lyons, William Flynn and Henry Talbot.

CHAPTER VI

Arson at Putnam Lodge Death of James Horgan

The torch is passed. Joseph Edward Kelley, Sr., who had come to Danvers on April 27, 1925, and reorganized the department leading it from the horse-drawn era to today's mechanical age, retired on January 26, 1958. He had had many uphill battles, for as we all know, change does not come easily, particularly in the fire service where tradition is so securely embedded. At best, it was very difficult for a stranger to come into a situation so entwined with relatives, friends, and mutual adventures from the past.

His first test had been the reorganization. It was successfully completed around 1929. His second and most severe test came during the Depression. The department did not lose any personnel then, but the pay of firefighters was reduced from $35.00 per week to $32.50. Later during the war years, he was tested because of the lack of manpower and the severe handicap of being unable to replace expended equipment. Joseph Kelley's finest achievements were accomplished soon after the war and continued until his retirement. In those years, our permanent manpower was increased fourfold and our apparatus was all of the latest design and in excellent condition. He had been chief for thirty-three years, an outstanding feat in itself. He represented the highest tradition of the fire service.

On the same day that Chief Kelley retired, John Joseph Farley was named the second permanent fire chief for the town of Danvers. Joe was not the first Farley to be a member of the department. His father, John, Sr., had been made a call man on May 1, 1907, assigned to Engine 3 and later appointed a call captain in May of 1923. He resigned on April 30, 1938.

John Joseph Farley served as Danvers Fire Chief from 1958 to 1973.

Joe's first formal introduction into the fire service was May 1, 1931, when he was appointed a call substitute. He replaced his dad as a permanent call man on May 1, 1938, and was assigned to Engine 3. Joe was given a leave of absence and joined the U.S. Army, April 9, 1942. Shortly after his discharge, he became a permanent man on June 1, 1946. When the first permanent civil service captains were appointed, he was one of them on January 11, 1952. Then, six years later, on a bleak, rainy January 26, 1958, Joe was summoned to the town hall where Town Manager Daniel J. McFadden swore him in as the second chief of the Danvers Fire Department. Though the climate that day was dismal, the rank and file members of the department were in a joyous mood, happy for Joe. Chief Kelley had done a memorable job as chief, and we all knew that Joe would continue on and lead us to become an even better department.

Joe Farley was known by every townie and held in the highest of respect. He had skipped several grades while in school. Upon his graduation from high school at the age of fifteen, he was too young to get a steady job. As a consequence, he had a very outstanding career as a baseball player for the old 'Port team in the Twilight League and also for some semi-pro teams.

Joe contributed many things to his new position. I can personally attest to this as we worked together for twenty-five years. He brought to the department his keen, intelligent foresight, the uncanny ability to see into people, but most of all, downright good common sense. He was never obvious outwardly as one in authority, but, by God, when he was there, you knew he was chief by his example, self-control, and air of confidence.

Chief Farley giving orders during a night fire.

This chief walked to work every morning and was in his office by eight o'clock. At times, he would permit someone to give him a ride home at five. Through Joe's leadership, we increased the permanent members to fifty-eight. We appointed eight lieutenants. The position of deputy chief was added then to the officer ranks. Joe Farley was a joy to work with. He was certainly an outstanding example for me when I became chief. I hope in my little way I left it better for someone else.

During Joe's fifteen year stewardship, he had many serious fires that challenged his firefighting expertise. In most instances, he was the victor. A few of those fires I will never forget. There was the night fire in 1958 at 6 Bridge

Street. It was about 2:30 a.m. All three rear porches of the three-decker were fully involved. I was on duty and called for a second alarm because of the life hazard and severity of the fire. Shortly thereafter, aid arrived from Beverly.

When Joe appeared on the scene, I related the actions I had taken and a few suggestions for future strategy. Then Joe told Dean Palmer, Chief of the Beverly Fire Department, so that everyone on that side of Spite Bridge could hear, "Marty has lost another one."

On May 14, 1959, Joseph E. Kelley died. The entire community mourned his passing. Local officials and the region's fire chiefs paid him many tributes for the contributions that he had made to Danvers and the fire service in general, for he had also been instrumental in organizing the Essex County Fire Chiefs' Association, a strong and moving force in fire protection. In this and in other ways he had been a far-sighted leader in his field. Chief Kelley had dedicated his life to the Danvers Fire Department.

In the same year, our fire alarm system, which had been installed in 1926, was completely replaced with a Gamewell system of the latest design. A generator now replaced the old lead batteries. The new system had ten circuits and was protected against lightning which in the past had caused considerable damage to the Central Fire Station. In the process all of the wooden schools in town were completely protected by sprinkler systems and master boxes connected to our fire alarm system. Charles Doyle, our fire alarm technician, supervised the transition from the old to the new.

Three commendations were awarded in 1959-1960. One was presented on June 16, 1959, to Firefighter Robert Osgood for his display of courage in rescuing a trapped employee of ViCliff's Restaurant on Route 114. Firefighter John M. Noonan of Engine 3 was commended also in 1959 for his swift action and initiative in closing a hard-to-reach propane valve under very hazardous conditions. I was recognized and granted three days off with pay for rescuing a thirteen year old girl from a house fire on Belgian Road in 1960.

The pay of the fire chief in 1959 was $6,200 and of a firefighter $4,700. The chief also received a new Ford, a station wagon, the first and only such vehicle for the department.

Part of the old Gamewell Fire Alarm Telegraph located at Central Fire Station.

Firefighter Robert Osgood had dashed into the burning ViCliff Restaurant to rescue a cook trapped in an upper room. Here firefighter C. Leonard Collins and Patrolman Edward J. Noonan administer oxygen from the department's portable resuscitator.

85

Firefighter Wilfred Vaillancourt tends the pump connection during the fire at ViCliff's Restaurant on Route 114 in June 1959.

On October 1, 1960 three tried-and-true men retired: call firefighter Bernard Lyons completed thirty-nine years; permanent firefighter William Ayers, thirty-one years; and permanent firefighter John D. Madison, also thirty-one years of dedicated service to the town of Danvers. Jack was a good man and a great firefighter, one of the best I ever had the privilege to know and to fight fires with.

These were years of rapid growth for Danvers. This is evidenced in the dramatic escalation in the number of requests for assistance. In 1961 the department responded to 530 local calls, over 3,000 inspections were made, and a total of 979 Christmas trees were sprayed with a retardant to discourage their ignition. We had been doing this last request for nearly ten years. We believed we were performing a worthwhile service to the community. But several federal agencies stated that our endeavors were nearly worthless. Consequently, this practice came to an end.

In 1962 the department responded to 555 calls. Then in 1963 because of new housing, the number jumped to 854 calls. That year our fire alarm system was extended to cover the entire Woodvale section of town for which the contractor reimbursed Danvers for the work and use of equipment.

A new American LaFrance one-thousand gallon, two-stage pump was delivered in November of 1962 at a cost of $23,505. It replaced our 1936 Pirsch which, in turn, had replaced our 1911 Knox Combination 1. For twenty-five years our Engine 4, a Pirsch six-hundred g.p.m., had been the backbone of our department and had worked at hundreds of fires never failing to perform as expected. It was now retired. Two new smoke ejectors were also purchased.

Chief Farley poses in front of the new 1962 American LaFrance pump.

In August of 1963, our most notorious arson fire occurred at the Putnam Lodge Restaurant on Summer Street, where a bold felon had placed about one dozen five-gallon glass jugs filled with gasoline throughout the lower portion of the building. He used a clock as a timing device and had professional fireworks fuses going from the mouth of one jug to that of another. The idea was that when the timer went off, the fuse was lit, then ignited the gasoline and broke the first jug of fuel and continued down the line. But in this case, after the initial container ignited, the fuse apparently fell off the second. Thus, only one jug was actually set on fire.

Captain Joseph Kelley, Jr., who lived two houses up the street from Putnam Lodge, was mowing his lawn when he looked up and saw billows of black smoke coming from the back of the structure. He ran across the street and pulled Box 216. I was the captain on duty. Upon arrival, I found the lower rear section completely enveloped in flames. I called for a second alarm as we began running lines in order to surround the fire and contain it.

It proved to be a stubborn blaze since the lower floor was cut up into several rooms. However, after about an hour, it was adequately knocked down so that we could advance into the ground floor. While we were extinguishing the fire in the partitions and other channels, call man Charles Pollard discovered the five-gallon jugs, which we capped and removed.

There followed a long and in-depth investigation conducted by the state fire marshal's office, Lieutenant Howard McDonald and Officer John Lyons of our police department, and me. Our study led us to southern New Hampshire. Well over one hundred people were interviewed. An inquest was then held, but our principal suspect had too many friends who provided him with an alibi. The case was never resolved.

Arson evidence, including gasoline filled bottles taken from the Putnam Lodge fire, is laid out at Central Fire Station.

Early in the spring of 1964, the New England Insurance Rating Association arrived in Danvers to make a thorough study of the town and its fire defenses as it had done previously in 1927 and 1936. Once again the department was as carefully scrutinized. The personnel were questioned and tested as to their competence in executing their duties and their knowledge of building construction and the general geography of the community. Taken into consideration also was the condition of our apparatus and the equipment used to combat fires and other emergency tasks as we are called upon to perform.

Our water supply and distribution system were investigated. More than sixty-five fire flow tests were conducted throughout Danvers. A fire flow test is done in this manner: we place a pressure gauge on one hydrant, and then we flow the next hydrant in the direction of the water leaving the second hydrant by the use of a pitot gauge. Then by means of a mathematical formula we can determine the amount of water available in various parts of the community. The results were again satisfactory.

Fortunately for Danvers our hydrants are very well situated. Basically they are at every intersection and five hundred feet apart. If a dead-end street is more than six hundred feet long, a main is run out to the hydrant.

As far as building construction and inspection are concerned, the Danvers Fire Department is unusual in that over the years from the inception of the position of building inspector, his duties and our fire prevention responsibilities merge in many sections of the law. However, both sides being mature and knowledgeable, we cooperate and complement one another. This has been true for the tenure of Pete Littlewood, our first inspector, of Roger Halle, of Willy Wright, and of Peter Bryson.

Another important aspect of the 1964 survey was that all involved agreed Engine 2 station in Tapleyville should be moved. A fire site committee was later formed with Donald F. Pelletier, chairman, and Ralph Ferguson, Hardy P. Wallace, Walter Cullen, and Francis M. Landolphi, members. I was assigned by Chief Farley to work with this group to represent the department.

During the first stage of the study, the chief and I visited over twenty newly built fire stations in the Boston area. We worked out a scheme whereby he would talk to the chief of the particular department we were checking out, and I would talk to the firefighters present. Thus we obtained the real truth as to the practicality of the building and its appurtenances.

At the same time, I reviewed very detailed maps of Danvers and the town's zoning by-laws as to where potential development could take place and consequently where the population might shift. At the time, it had been determined exactly the route that highway I-95 would take. After several months of work, I proposed to the chief that Engine 2 should be set on a one-acre plot on the southeast portion of the Danvers State Hospital property. The rating bureau overwhelmingly approved the site. Later this parcel was purchased for the price of $1.00 from the Commonwealth.

After over a year of construction, the new station was ready for occupancy. In the early morning of October 23, 1967, the door of the one hundred twenty-

The new Engine 2 station off Maple Street in Hathorne was opened for service in 1967.

Elden Swindell sits in the two horse hitch pung filled with hose and gear in this ca. 1902 winter view of the ca. 1844 **General Scott** *Engine 2 house located at 59 Holten Street.*

four year old Engine 2 station on Holten Street was opened for the last time. At 9:19 a.m., Engine 2 reported by vocal alarm that the men were in the new station on Maple Street. This marked the end of an era for Tapleyville and a beginning for Hathorne. Once an average of twenty-seven trains a day had passed over the crossing on Holten Street, but like the horse and buggy, trains here are a thing of the past. What had been needed was a more useful and practical location, and Ferncroft was the logical choice.

The rating association further recommended that the position of deputy chief be established; that company officers should be on duty at all times in the outlying stations; and that the structure of the department should consist of a chief, a deputy chief, four captains and eight lieutenants. The department would then have four groups or teams with a captain in charge of each and a lieutenant at every outlying station. The recommended number of personnel in each group would be twenty, including officers and men.

This 1951 photograph taken from almost the same location as the one at left shows the nineteenth century Engine 2 fire house slightly modified but still in use. Members of the company in their turn-out gear, including C. Leonard Collins, Edward Ferguson and Roland Sturtevant (on back step from left to right), pose with their new American LaFrance one thousand g.p.m. pump.

    Over the next few years department personnel were increased. Charles Collins was appointed a captain. Named permanent firefighters were Richard C. Wessell, Richard T. Pyburn, and Anthony D. Santorella. Two new positions were created to improve the running of the department. Firefighter Francis O. Maynard became firefighter/mechanic, and Firefighter Charles H. Doyle was appointed firefighter/fire alarm technician.

    In 1968, the position of deputy chief was finally initiated. Previously, in the early part of this century, there had been two call deputy fire chiefs: Clarence Dennett in the 'Port and William Berry in the Plains. During the reorganization period of the 1920s, the town dropped the position. Then, following the recommendation of this latest rating survey, an examination for the position was held. Town Manager Robert E. Curtis appointed me the first deputy fire chief. My

Smoke billows from the Your Market fire in August 1965.

principal duties were to be responsible for the training of the members of the department and to be the chief officer in the absence of the chief.

A giant step forward was made on January 17, 1969. Six permanent lieutenants were named to the department: Arnold L. Cyr, Robert J. Cyr, Theodore Foster, James McInnis, Richard Sullivan, and Richard C. Wessell. Now the department had a lieutenant and two firefighters at both Engines 2 and 3. The total complement of the department was forty-four.

Finally, the 1964 survey recommended a new four-bay fire headquarters at a location to be determined in the near future and that a separate radio frequency be given the department. [Construction on the new Central Fire Station began in 1994 on High Street. It was dedicated the following year on Sunday, October 1.]

Let me return now to other matters that occurred in 1965. Lieutenant Jeremiah Minnehan of the Danvers Police Department lived in the second floor apartment above Your Market, a grocery store at 73 Holten Street. About dawn on a very mild August morning, a passerby spotted flames coming from the stairway leading up to Jerry's flat and pulled Box 224 at the corner of Pine and Holten. Upon the arrival of Engine 1, Acting Captain Robert Osgood saw that the flames had made rapid headway up and into that apartment. On the first floor, the store itself was set afire when the stairshaft caved in.

The main body of the fire was attacked from the sidewalk. It became apparent early on that the forces at hand could not adequately cope with the situation.

Bob ordered the sounding of a second alarm, summoning help from Middleton, Beverly, and Peabody with Salem covering at headquarters. Chief Farley soon was on the scene. Despite the efforts of over fifty firefighters, the store was completely gutted. On the bright side, thanks to the Your Market owners, we had several months' supply of free coffee and other canned goods.

Other changes in the ranks occurred in 1965. Captain Ronald F. Sturtevant and Firefighter George E. Jones, Jr. retired. Charles Collins was named captain. In September a new three-quarter ton pick-up truck was purchased at a cost of $2,015.26 and referred to as Squad 1.

Earlier in the year on April 4, 1965, the whole town, but especially the fire department, had been terribly shocked at the death of Firefighter James Horgan. Jim was a well-respected member of our department. His life's dream had been to be a firefighter.

I was the captain in charge at headquarters when we received a telephone call for a grass fire behind the Danvers Plaza adjacent to Route 1 in Hathorne. Responding to this alarm along with me and John Noonan was Jimmy Horgan, with whom I had joined the department in 1947. It should have been a simple, routine job for us.

At the scene we found a brisk grass fire in progress. We ran a booster line up the slight embankment and attacked the blaze from that point. Jimmy, using a broom, was off to our right. The next thing I heard was Firefighter Noonan, who was operating the pump, yell to me to return to the engine. When I did, I found Jimmy sitting on the front running board gasping for breath.

We immediately laid him on the ground, made him as comfortable as possible, and called for an ambulance. En route to the hospital, he lost consciousness twice, so we attempted resuscitation. At the emergency room he was attended to by the doctors and nurses present, but to no avail. James Horgan, who loved his job, literally died with his boots on.

The old Marshall's Harness Shop on School Street is fully engulfed in flames during the January 1967 fire.

CHAPTER VII

School Street Inferno The End of Parker's Gristmill

What goes around, comes around as I said before. Things do seem to progress in a circular fashion. Slow times are followed by busy years only to be succeeded again by slow ones. 1966 was a quiet year. One of the main programs was the complete revamping of our mutual aid pact with other communities in southern Essex County. We also established a practice that Engines 2 and 3 would handle the mutual aid calls and not Engine 1.

Nineteen sixty-seven made up for 1966, and then some. On a cold, drizzly Sunday, January 9 at 12:55 p.m., a passerby observed smoke coming from the rear storage shed of Max Berry's carpentry shop at 6 to 8 School Street and ran to pull nearby Box 13. This complex, approximately 177 years old, was composed of three structures: the office and carpentry shops of William A. Berry and Son, General Contractors; the one-time harness shop of Edwin S. Marshall, previously Charles McTernen's; and the lumber storage shed attached to the rear of the harness shop. There was a narrow alley separating the Berry property from Ernest S. Richardson's large barn used then as a warehouse by J. A. Mercier Plumbing Supply at 10 School Street.

Captain Joseph E. Kelley, Jr. was the officer in charge at headquarters. Upon leaving the station, he saw smoke rising above School Street, for even then the complex was burning furiously. His men rapidly laid a line from the corner of Maple and School Streets and proceeded down School to a point just beyond the fire. While the others in the company were putting the supply line into the pump and also readying the deck gun, Joe went down the alley to assess the situation. He returned to Engine 1 and ordered the striking of a second alarm. Later a third was sounded. This brought assistance from Beverly, Salem, Middleton, Ipswich, Manchester, Lynn, and Swampscott. Within a few minutes sufficient manpower had assembled at the scene.

A four-man unit from Engine 4 took the deck gun down the alleyway. The placement of this gun was of acute strategic importance as it would cut off the spread of fire between the shed and the Richardson barn less than eight feet away. This action was part of a pre-conceived plan of Chief Farley's in case this

Leading a contingent of the Danvers Fire Department up Elm Street in the 1963 Memorial Day Parade is Chief Joe Farley (white hat, center), Captain Joseph E. Kelley, Jr. (at right), and Leland E. Martin, Jr. (at left). Among those men in their dress uniform are Arnold Cyr, Charles Doyle, Theodore Foster, James Horgan, Robert Joyce, Alfred Kuell, Charles Kuell, George LaChance, and Henry Talbot.

property ever caught fire. He had discussed it with the men, but had not had time to put it into practice.

I was at home that noontime and promptly responded when I heard Joe Kelley over my portable radio say, "Smoke showing," as he left the station. Jeffrey, my son, who was eleven years old, accompanied me. Upon our arrival, Joe asked me to assist in getting the aerial ladder pipe into operation in order to pour water down into the buildings from an elevated position. Later Captain Kelley credited the electric light department with quickly cutting off the power on the overhead lines carrying 4,100 volts. While those lines were alive, Joe told reporter Bill Cahill, "It was no picnic fooling around with ladders."

Soon Chief Farley himself was on the scene supervising the overall fireground situation, making certain that the area was completely surrounded by hand lines, deck guns, and ladder pipes, and that the outside sprinkler system in the Richardson property had been activated. At a time when all the water we were pouring into the fire seemed to be making no impression, an off-duty captain reported to the chief for instructions and said that in his opinion the conflagration could only be stopped when it got down to Oak Street. With that bit of free advice, Joe Farley got his real Irish stubborness up; and with his skills, the determination of several dozen firefighters and the will of the good Lord, the fire never crossed the alley, even when two vehicles parked inside the buildings exploded sending fiery embers everywhere.

It was a spectacular inferno with flames, at one time, shooting up as much as one hundred feet into the air. Fortunately as perilous as the situation had been for the men down the alleyway with the deck gun, there was no loss of life. But it was a close call. When the middle of the harness shop began to buckle, Joe Kelley ordered his men out of there. I clearly recall that Walt Skinner and Frank Maynard were at the deck gun, and there were others.

The loss from this fire was estimated to be in the vicinity of $150,000. The total could have been higher had not the owners of Diaphragm Industries, Inc. at R75 Maple Street had a solid twenty-foot high cement block firewall erected between their property and that of Max Berry. This fire protection measure saved their small factory from certain destruction. Still the havoc that two young boys who set the fire brought upon School Street was devastating. Firemen had to remain at the site for twenty-four hours to be sure that the fire could not be rekindled.

Marshall's Harness Shop, where the "Senate" had assembled, was completely gone. It was a sad loss. Here many fine old conservative Danvers men had met informally on a daily basis and discussed the problems of the town. Among these oldsters I am proud to say, in the 1920s, was my grandfather George B. Sanford. He had lived nearly all his life in Danvers and had been a conductor on the electric car lines.

Besides these three structures being destroyed that year, the Richard Barry Block on High Street between the Danvers Savings Bank and the old Orpheum Theatre was gutted on September 7. Some readers may remember one shop that had been here—Michelson's Candy Store, a real palace of sweets. The fire got started in a pizza parlor, quickly entered the cockloft, and spread throughout the adjoining stores necessitating three alarms to bring it under control.

This year also marked the end of another nostalgic era for the Danvers Fire Department. Joseph E. Kelley, Jr. had become a call man in 1938 and after serving three and a half years in the U.S. Air Force, he returned home. In 1946, he was appointed a permanent member of the department. In 1952, after passing the examination for captain, and by the way, topping

In this 1950s photo Firefighter Walton F. "Walt" Skinner sits aboard the 1936 Engine 4. Skinner began as a call fireman in 1927. He remained with the department until 1969, always believing that the most important job of the fireman was to help people.

the list, he was named to that post. Over the years we had fought all kinds of fires together, but the rigors of firefighting left him with deteriorating health, and so after twenty-nine years, he transferred, during the fall of 1967, to the town hall and became our assistant town manager.

The year 1967 also marked the beginning of the fire science program at North Shore Community College. I, with many other firefighters from the area, enrolled in the fall for the first semester. For me, this was the start of a long and happy association. As for the department, we had thirty-eight full-time firefighters in 1967 and twelve call men. Our budget was $289, 374. The chief's salary was $9,000; captain's pay, $8,000; and a firefighter's, $6,500.

In 1969 we lost some long-time firefighters. Walton F. Skinner retired after forty-two faithful years as call and permanent man. Walt was a great ballplayer in his younger days. His father had been a call firefighter, and his brother Hollis was one of our permanent men in the 1920s and 1930s. Walt had two sons who became members of the department: Mike and Ron Skinner. Raymond J. Guppy, who served thirty-eight years as a call and permanent firefighter, retired also. Appointed firefighters were William Graves and Robert LaPointe.

In February of 1969, a new one hundred foot aerial was delivered from Peter Pirsch and Sons. The department had drawn up extensive and detailed specifications for this ladder truck in 1967. Pirsch had built our 1936 Engine 4 and our 1947, sixty-five foot aerial. The latter engine was now placed in reserve.

This new ladder arrived in town late on a Thursday afternoon. It went directly to Engine 2, where it was stationed that night. The following morning, Lester Metcalf arrived in town as the representative from the manufacturer. He instructed the members of the department in the operation of the vehicle. Chief Farley and I, accompanied by several other men, went to Engine 2 about 9:00 a.m. to inspect the new truck.

After that it was time to drive the new ladder truck. Lester gave me the privilege. Several of us got on it. We proceeded out of Engine 2 and down Maple Street toward the Square. We made a wide circle as far up as Greenleaf Drive, back onto Summer Street and back to Maple.

When we had been drawing up the specifications for the vehicle, there was a great deal of concern as to whether or not it would fit into the central station. Therefore, we had the door widened as much as possible (eight inches), but the height of the door had to remain the same. We asked the help of the town engineer who had cooperated by shooting "grades" that we could determine the maximum height that the vehicle could be as it was backed up the ramp and then onto the level floor of the station.

Now as I slowed down and turned the corner from Maple Street onto Locust, there was quite a large group of men waiting to see if the Pirsch would fit. I asked Lester if he would back it in, and he emphatically declined. I am not the world's best driver by any means, but I took a deep breath and said, "Here goes nothing." With the able assistance of the tillerman operating the steering wheel at the rear of the long truck, I drove the ladder into the parking lot across the street, put the transmission into reverse, and said to my Friend upstairs, "Please let it fit."

Traffic was stopped on Locust as we proceeded very cautiously and carefully to back the ladder into the station. We did it that first time with less than 1 1/2" clearance between the windshield of the tillerman and the first carrying beam in the ceiling. I turned off the ignition and never drove it again.

Extensive work was done on our fire alarm system in 1970 due to the construction of Route I-95, under which our cables now pass in conduit. The system

The old Parker Grain Mill building on Water Street in enveloped in flames during a spectacular evening fire in December 1970.

was also extended to the Liberty Tree Mall, where over the next few years several new master boxes were installed.

On December 2, 1970, fire destroyed one of our early landmarks, the eighteenth-century gristmill built by Archelaus and John Putnam. It was located on Water Street just over the Szypko Bridge. Many readers will remember it as the George H. Parker Grain Co.

Within twelve minutes it became a general alarm conflagration. The difficulty here was that the fire could only be attacked from one side as the river prevented surrounding the building. One of the cardinal principals of firefighting is "locate, surround, confine and extinguish" the fire. It was impossible here. The result was that in a few hours Parker's was reduced to ashes. The remaining section was torn down a few days later. Numerous small fires had been extinguished

Above: A view of the 1970 Parker Grain fire from the Crane River.

previously here, but, of course, it was open to vandals. Thus ended our last gristmill. An historic structure had surrendered to the flames.

In 1971, this department saw many changes in personnel and equipment. In March a new 1250 g.p.m. Ward LaFrance pump was delivered to us. While both Ward LaFrance and American LaFrance are located in Elmira, New York, they are two different companies. This vehicle was unique for two reasons. It was the first "Ward" fire truck the department had

Below: "Moby Dick," the white Ward LaFrance pump purchased in 1971, and the 1969 Pirsch one hundred foot aerial Ladder 1 in action on July 9, 1972, at a fire at the Jones Boys warehouse on Water Street.

100

Firefighters Bob Osgood and Bill Murphy, responding to a 1971 fire at Creese and Cook Leather factory on Water Street, dress the hydrant.

purchased, and it was painted WHITE. Before the vehicle had made its first response, it was nicknamed "Moby Dick."

Over the years, we had had literally dozens of fires at the sprawling Creese and Cook leather factory on Water Street. One of these fires occurred on March 13, 1971, at about 2:30 p.m. A motor in an exhaust duct situated between the fourth floor and the roof became ignited and, in turn, set fire to the lacquer residue it was exhausting.

I ordered the striking of a second alarm and the aerial thrown to the roof. I then ascended the ladder followed by Lieutenant (now Captain) Arnold Cyr. A local newspaper reported what happened next:

> A squad of firemen defied flames and heavy black smoke yesterday afternoon to save the life of the deputy fire chief after the roof of the four-story leather factory burst into a ball of fire.
> Deputy Chief Leland Martin was approaching an exhaust shaft at the Creese and Cook plant to determine the extent of a fire burning there when the section of the roof between him and the aerial ladder exploded into flames.
> Firemen, led by Lt. Arnold Cyr, stayed at the edge of the roof with a small hoseline until the deputy could escape.

101

On May 27, 1971, nine new firefighters were named to the department bringing the total complement to fifty-eight officers and men. Those appointed were Jeffrey Harrison, Rusty Smith, Arnold Weeks, Jr., John Pettipas, Albert Petronzio, Alan Weeks, Gerry Mills, James Tutko, and George Snow. These men got their jobs in anticipation of the reduction in hours of the work week for firefighters voted at the annual town meeting of 1970. April 18 at 8:00 a.m. was the beginning of the new work week. From 1951 to this date, we had been working a fifty-six hour week. In June, a new General Motors Corp. 3/4 ton pickup truck was delivered to replace Squad 1.

Of the many events that occurred in 1972, two things unfortunately are outstanding. On the afternoon of June 5, a gasoline tractor trailer carrying 11,900 gallons of fuel failed to negotiate the curve going from Route 1 onto Route 95. The heavy rig rolled over several times, finally coming to rest on its side and bursting into a volcano of flame. The driver escaped, but was severely burned and succumbed to his injuries a few days later.

Upon Chief Farley's arrival at the scene of the fire, he had struck a second alarm to which Middleton responded. We laid a line of hose from North Street nearly a mile away, and immediately started applying foam on the fire. We had to transmit a request for all the foam in the area because our supply was insufficient for a fire of this magnitude. A request was also made to Logan Airport and to the Pease Air Force Base in New Hampshire for additional foam trucks.

The fire burned with great rapidity and gave off tremendous amounts of heat. We had to use two foam lines simultaneously, employing a V formation and relieving the nozzle men frequently. Apparently we did make a successful attack and extinguished the flames. (Actually, we do not know whether we doused the fire or if the fuel was consumed.)

The Texaco Oil Company, owner of the tractor trailer, replaced the foam that had been expended. At the July meeting of the Essex County Fire Chiefs, I proposed that we initiate a foam bank which was started soon after. The idea is that every community donates five gallons of foam per each 5,000 population with a minimum of a five-gallon donation. In 1981 the supply was divided between Haverhill and Danvers. As of this writing, it has run successfully for nearly twenty years. Many times we have been called upon to deliver foam from this bank stored at Engine 2.

On December 5, 1972, a very serious fire struck the Almy's Department Store at the Danvers Plaza. There were approximately two hundred shoppers and sales personnel in the store who had to be evacuated, an action that delayed firefighting operations. Eventually this mid-morning blaze went to five alarms, but it was confined to the back storage area.

This fire had started in stacked boxes of yarn making it very difficult for the water from the sprinklers to reach the seat of the conflagration. The heat became so intense that a twelve-inch steel carrying beam pushed its way through the rear brick wall due to expansion. To give you an idea of the magnitude of the blaze, a total of twenty-one sprinkler heads throughout the store had fused or gone into operation.

A lighter aspect here began with the arrival of Chief Dean Palmer of Beverly shortly after eleven o'clock. When things were being brought under control around noon, he and Joe Farley went to lunch. A few minutes after they arrived

A tractor trailer truck filled with about 12,000 gallons of gasoline overturned at Route I-95 on June 5, 1972. The driver died from his injuries several days later.

at the York Steak House on Endicott Street, they were enjoying their meal, when a Mrs. Madden from the 'Port rushed up to Joe and excitedly told him about the very serious fire at Almy's. Joe calmly remarked, "Marty's there. After we eat, we'll check it out."

Another first this year was the purchase of a new Ford LTD chief's car that cost $7,999. It was the first to be painted yellow.

At 8:00 a.m. on April 1, 1973, the work week was reduced from forty-eight to forty-two hours. The structure of the department now consisted of a chief, deputy chief, and four groups each with one captain, two lieutenants, and eleven men. On May 7, a new Ward LaFrance was placed in service. It was a 1250 g.p.m. single-stage pump with a three hundred gallon booster tank. The cost was $51,698, and it was painted lime yellow. The previous Engine 1, "Moby Dick," was now renumbered Engine 3.

Engine 7, the 1930s converted Chevrolet truck used as a grass fire vehicle, sits inside Engine house 3 in this 1960s photograph. A favorite mascot of the firefighters was Duke the Dog, a Dalmatian who accompanied engines to fire responses. Duke rests here by the front doors. Upon his death, Duke was buried on the engine house property.

CHAPTER VIII

Chelsea and Lynn Burn Nesson Block Gutted

Once again the time had arrived to pass the torch of leadership. On Friday, August 31, 1973, Joseph Farley left the station for the last time as Chief of the Danvers Fire Department. I drove Joe home that afternoon. It was a quiet ride and a sad one, for a long and lustrous career was coming to an end. Joe had done a lot for his department in his fifteen-year tenure and thirty-eight years as call and permanent firefighter. He was responsible for purchasing many pieces of equipment to keep us equal to or better than most other communities. Joe was quiet, honest, and down-to-earth. In many ways he had helped me. Primarily he kept me reined in as at times I know I must have been a little too ambitious, but he was a good mentor, and I always had the highest respect for him.

On Saturday, September 1, then town manager Robert E. Curtis appointed me Acting Chief of the Danvers Fire Department. I remained in that capacity until the final grades were made known from the examination held in May of 1972. I was the high scorer, and so became the third permanent chief of the department on November 20, 1973.

My short swearing-in ceremony took place in the front lobby of the Hunt Memorial Hospital on Lindall Hill. Joe Kelley, Jr. was confined there, recovering from a serious operation. I picked up Bob Curtis at the town hall and proceeded to the hospital where Joe was waiting for us. After a brief exchange of old fire tales, Joe pinned the gold badge of chief on my uniform.

Sunday, October 14, was a beautiful fall day. The sun shone brightly, and the wind came from the west. Spark that I am, this day was to hold one of the greatest experiences of my life. At 3:58 p.m., an alarm was sounded for a fire started by youngsters in a Chelsea junkyard. Despite the valiant efforts of the first arriving company, it soon became overwhelming and out of control. A second alarm had to be struck, followed by many more until finally at 6:30 p.m. a teletyped message requesting all available help was sent from the Chelsea Police Department to every area police department.

Danvers Engines 4 and C-1 went to Chelsea with nine firefighters. Leaving the station, we could see the smoke in the western sky. It was an eerie feeling driving down Route 1 without any other vehicles in sight as all traffic in both directions had been detoured because of the conflagration.

As we approached Chelsea, we were directed to a marshalling area in front of the Chelsea fire headquarters. From there we were dispatched with a pilot to First Street, where we laid a line into our deck gun and another line was supplied us from a Lowell pump. We could only stay here twenty minutes as the fire was approaching our position very rapidly. With the assistance of several dozen bystanders, we literally picked up the deck gun with the hose still intact and relocated about one block away. Here we remained all night. About 10:30 the following morning, we were relieved and returned to Danvers.

The loss was more than $100,000,000. Over a thousand people were homeless. That fire totally destroyed eighteen city blocks and several dozen other structures. One more block to the west and it would have endangered the Tobin Bridge. As it was, you could not touch the railings of the bridge without burning your hands because of the radiant heat. There were over two thousand firefighters from eighty departments working at the fire. This was my first experience with a conflagration of this magnitude. It was not to be my last.

As previously noted, the first North Shore Community College Fire Science Degree Program started in 1967. As you recall I was in that first class. Then following the retirement of Chief Farley, I had relinquished my studies so that I could devote all my time to studying for the chief's examination. In my particular case, that meant a minimum of six hours a day.

When I returned to college in the fall of 1973, I found that a new course had been added to the program, Tactics and Strategy. Joe O'Keefe, later the state fire marshal, was then head of the program. He had been diligently looking for a teacher for the course. After months of searching, he asked District Chief Jim Scollins of the Lynn Fire Department and me to be the instructors.

Chief Martin confers with Captain Robert Joyce during a fire on Stone Street on February 24, 1974.

I began my teaching career that fall and continued for the next twelve years. I found this work to be very demanding, but at the same time, very rewarding. I taught over six hundred officers and firefighters Tactics and Strategy. Ironically, this course is a required one for a degree in the program; however, the dean of studies did not want to give Jim and me the four credits even though we taught the course. It was only by the intervention of President Harold Shively that we were awarded our credits.

The next two years, 1974 and 1975, were quiet ones. The former year will be remembered as the one of promotions. Lieutenant Richard Wessell was promoted to deputy chief to fill the vacancy I had left. I've always counted him a loyal friend and a true credit to the department. Lieutenants Richard Sullivan and Arnold Cyr became captains and firefighters Joseph Santorella, Michael Skinner, and David C. Sullivan were promoted to lieutenants. As far as fires were concerned, we had a very serious one at Babco Industries at 28 Water Street in March. A portion of the building was completely gutted. The overheating of oxygen and acetylene containers caused many explosions.

Aftermath of a fatal plane crash on Massachusetts Avenue in Woodvale near the approach to Beverly Airport on December 21, 1976.

Our major emphasis in 1975 was putting the inspection program on a regular basis, whereby "in-service" inspections were made daily, both in the morning and the afternoon, so that everyone became familiar with all industrial and commercial properties in town.

The year 1976 was when budget cuts were called for by the finance committee. It was suggested that eight men be cut from our department and replaced by ten call men. Since our workload was increasing every year for both actual fires and inspection work, a cut in manpower could have been disastrous. It was also suggested the Engine 3 on High Street be closed. This engine company traditionally responded to more alarms than any other company in Danvers. The finance committee hearings this year were just a rattling of the chains. Nothing changed, but we would hear more of this in 1981.

On December 21, 1976, a bitterly cold day, a two-engine airplane with two people aboard was flying from Bangor, Maine, to Boston when it developed engine trouble. The plane landed at Beverly Airport so as to have a mechanic correct the problem. After he had examined one of the engines, he told the pilot he would have to repair the carburetor, a job that would take a few hours.

The pilot and his passenger, anxious to get to Boston, decided to have the repairs done at Logan. They took off, but when they were attempting to gain altitude, the trouble began again. The pilot altered his course and tried to return to Beverly. As he was making his approach, he suddenly lost altitude. His landing gear struck a power line on Massachusetts Avenue with the result that the airplane crashed into a house. The two flyers were instantly killed, and the plane was entirely consumed in the ensuing fire.

During 1977, our department went through troubled times in negotiations. We had been nearly three years without a contract when the Memorial Day parade was held. Because of a dispute between management (of which I was a part) and the firefighters, the union opted not to have the chief march with them. As I stood there in the middle of Sylvan Street after being told this, many thoughts flashed through my mind. I had but two options, either to go home with my disappointment or to march alone. I am, as I said, a veteran on World War II, and so I chose to march alone. And march I did! That day I was six feet tall.

As for salaries at the time, I was earning $24,800, and firefighters, $12,400.

During the latter part of 1977 and then 1978, we had a series of fires in the Highlands section of town. We were sure that we had an arsonist, but a definite pattern could not be fixed. At 4:35 a.m. on May 28, a fire was discovered in the eighty-seven year old First Church building at the corner of Centre and Hobart Street. It had been set at two separate locations in the hallway between the front and rear doors. Initially Firefighter Arnold Weeks, neighbor Richard Trask, and I were able to carefully enter the smoke-filled church in order to save silver communion vessels and other objects. The loss was approximately $300,000.

Devastation of the 1890 First Church, Congregational sanctuary as the result of an arson fire in May 1978.

On the morning of the disastrous fire, which was a Sunday, the Reverend William Conway held services on the front lawn. Though not completely destroyed, the church was torn down, and then it was born again. Like a Phoenix, the church has risen from the ashes five times on that site. Dedication services were held at 3:00 p.m. on September 28, 1980.

108

Nineteen seventy-nine was another year for a first. We purchased and put into service our first commercial chassis fire truck, a Ford C8000 built by Continental Fire Trucks of Hopkinton. It is a diesel with an automatic transmission, a one-thousand gallon single-stage pump, and a five hundred gallon booster tank. This pump was placed in service at headquarters and designated Engine 1. It is now (1990) presently designated Engine 4 and is a reserve pump at headquarters. This was the first of two commercial chassis that we have purchased, the other being Engine 3 on High Street.

In my experience, these vehicles have not met the needs of our department. The main reason is that the cab design is built for a commercial dump truck and not for firefighters with full protective gear and an air pack. The bucket seats are much too small for a fully equipped man. While these trucks may prove perfectly all right in other departments, they definitely do not meet our needs, and I would not recommend the purchase of a commercial vehicle again. The cost of this piece of apparatus was $56,462. For $8,266 we also bought a one-ton General Motors pickup to serve as a new squad vehicle.

There emerged in 1979 the first thoughts of building a new station and joining headquarters with Engine 3 at a location in the vicinity of High Street and Bayview Avenue. One parcel that was seriously considered was where the Danvers BMW car dealership is now. This site is over an acre, but the previous owner had signed a purchase and sales agreement the week before I spoke with her. Just to add one more disappointment to the year, this was the time I went head-to-head with the residents of Longbow Road and Seneca Drive before the planning board. The neighbors were vehemently opposed to a connector road I wanted between Summer and Locust Streets. I lost that battle. I was against dead-end streets then; I always will be because of their restricted access.

Nineteen seventy-nine brought down the curtain on the careers of two veteran firefighters. I was quoted as saying the *Salem Evening News* of June 18, "The double retirement of Firefighters Francis Dwinell and John Noonan has severed the last of the ties with the old department." These men had entered the department before World War II. They were good firemen, loyal and true, and I miss them both. We fought many fires together, and I gained a lot of experience being in their company.

The year 1980 arrived and left like a sleeping dog on a hot summer's day. Our inspection program was completely rewritten, and new procedures were initiated by Deputy Wessell. All places of business that held an innholder's license were scheduled for quarterly inspections. We had a very dry spring and consequently we had several hundred grass and wood fires and most, if not all, of our 1 1/8" hose was destroyed.

Over the years we have built the department from one permanent firefighter, George E. Jones, Sr., in 1911 to a total, in 1981, of fifty-eight men and officers. During the review of my budget, the town manager informed me that I would have to cut it by approximately $225,000. The only way that this amount of money could be realized was to reduce our manpower as 97 percent of our budget is for salaries and wages. Fortunately due to a quirk of fate, four men retired, a fifth took a voluntary leave of absence and three more firefighters made it known that they would retire before the end of the year. Thus no one had to be let go, but that year our department lost eight members through retirement or resignation. The result of this drastic cut of 14 percent of our force was that we had to reduce the number of men at Engines 2 and 3 from three to two per shift. The real truth is that in the two outlying stations, reduction in manpower was 33 1/3 percent. I never believed that this would happen, but Proposition 2 1/2 was voted on and approved, and this was the result of that vote.

After having fought the great forest fire in Sanford, Maine, in 1953 and the great Chelsea conflagration in 1973, I really believed that I had seen the last of the great fires in my career. But on the morning of November 28, I found that I was totally wrong in that assumption. Shortly after 3:55 a.m., we received a call from Beverly control that Lynn had struck a fifth alarm and that we should respond to the vicinity of the Edison Hotel. Engine 3 was immediately dispatched. I went to headquarters and picked up two more firefighters and reported to Lynn. Upon our arrival, I met Joe Scanlon, chief of the Lynn Fire Department, and the one with whom I had taught at North Shore Community College. Both of us had studied together either on Tuesday or Thursday nights from 7:00 to 10:00 p.m. for more than twenty-five years under the tutelage of Chief John Clougherty of Boston. He was a terrific firefighter and a wonderful father of thirteen children. His son, John, Jr., became a deputy chief on the Boston Fire Department.

Joe now directed us to set up Engine 3 at a hydrant in front of the Vamp Building. Shortly before this, I had called back to Danvers and requested four more firefighters to come to the scene. The fire at this point was raging completely out of control, and it seemed nearly impossible that mere men and their engines could halt the spread of the giant sheet of flame that now confronted us. Not every building in its path was destroyed as the fire jumped and went around some structures to ignite another building half a block away.

An example of how strange this fire advanced was the Benson shoe factory, an eight-story brick and wood-frame building. It was a full block from the fire, but a flying ember ignited a wooden window shutter on the third floor. I was standing beside Chief John Quinn of Nahant when we saw it happen. We rushed to the rear of the factory and mustered a company of about ten or twelve firefighters. We forced open the door and advanced a two and a half inch line up the stairshaft, which was of "scissor" design and completely enclosed from the first to the top floor. Somehow in the confusion and darkness, smoke and heat, the lead man inadvertently went to the fourth floor. I stayed at the base and encouraged the men in advancing the line.

By this time, they had gone a good seventy-five feet onto the fourth floor when they realized that they were above the fire which was spreading rapidly. The flames were being fed by oil-soaked floors and flimsy interior partitions. I heard a lot of confusion and shouting in the airshaft and went up. I met Chief Quinn on the landing of the third floor. He was nearly trapped there, but he had been assisted out by the heroic efforts of Michael Borsetti of the Beverly Fire Department, who later received a high commendation from Chief Palmer.

I now ordered the men on the fourth floor to go back down the stairs to the third floor. We attacked the fire from the landing but soon realized that we could not hold our position, so we retreated and tried to fight the fire from the roof of an adjoining building. At about 9:00 a.m., the rear portion of the factory collapsed into a tremendous pile of bricks and rubble sending flames and brands hundreds of feet into the air. We worked in this general area until about 4:00 p.m. when we were dismissed as the fire had practically burned itself out.

Comparing the two conflagrations, Chelsea and Lynn, the former's fire involved two and three story structures. The flames did leap across the streets but not too high into the air due to the lack of wind. But in Lynn the buildings were six and eight stories high. Driven by the wind, the flames leaped into the air nearly as high as the tallest buildings. I sincerely hoped that this would be my last conflagration, but the worst for me was yet to come. At that Lynn fire, six firefighters were injured from falling debris. A total of eighty-two departments responded with more than six hundred men. Over one and a half miles of the city were completely burned out, and over seven hundred fifty people were left homeless.

For new equipment in the years 1981–1982, Danvers Motor Company loaned us a car for the deputy fire chief. It was only used for fire prevention activities and did not respond to emergencies. The next year our second commercial chassis engine arrived. It was another Ford C8000 modified by Emergency One Fire Apparatus Manufacturer in Ocala, Florida, a division of Federal Signal Company. In addition to custom work, the firm was the first to use heavy-duty extruded aluminum and aluminum plate. The price for our engine was $89,891.

On August 20, 1982, another disastrous fire devastated Danvers Square. This one apparently started in the Supreme Roast Beef Shop at 6 Elm Street in the old Nesson Block. It spread rapidly by way of the cockloft to Connelly's Candy Store which had opened only eight days before. It also gutted the Siesta Sleep Shop. This fire had been reported sometime after 4:00 a.m. by Steve Piccolo working in his shoe repair shop across the street. He noticed smoke coming from the sandwich shop. Quite quickly this fire went from a first to a second and then to a general alarm. Seven other communities helped us in combatting the flames.

We had had a series of three fires in this block before it was finally torn down. All three were of suspicious origin. We spent several weeks investigating them with the assistance of the state fire marshal's office. Our leads wound up in dead ends because no one involved was willing to take a polygraph test. Today, the Atrium at the corner of Elm and High Streets stands on the site.

On August 1, 1982, Lieutenant Michael Skinner was appointed our first full-time Fire Prevention Officer. This position was a challenge to Michael from day one, but his skills in fire prevention work have been brought to the point where I have let him handle all the plan reviews and inspections of Rosewood IV, a twelve-story office building off of Route 114.

Education was much on our minds this year. Massachusetts had a complete reorganization of its higher education institutions. All colleges and universities were to be administered by a board of trustees. I had the very high distinction of being appointed a member of the first board of trustees of North Shore Community College, from which I had graduated in 1974. I was reappointed to a second term and was very proud to give of my time and whatever talents I had to offer. Being a trustee, I could not, of course, teach at North Shore, so I submitted by resignation to President George Traicoff, and my teaching career ended.

A third promotion for a member of the Danvers Fire Department occurred when Town Manager Wayne Marquis pinned a captain's badge on Robert Cyr, who then became the commanding officer of Group 4.

This photo exhibits a deck gun in action. Here Firefighter Robert Gilmore directs its use during a 1970 fire.

CHAPTER IX

Local Heroes Cited For Bravery

In late February of 1983, members of the Danvers Fire Department experienced the most harrowing, life-threatening experience of their careers. At approximately 10:12 p.m. a twelve thousand gallon propane tank truck began off-loading its cargo at the Ventron plant on Andover Street. The vapor recovery line became disconnected permitting the escape of the gas which drifted into the boiler room and promply exploded, thereby parting the liquid line resulting in a tremendous fire.

When I left my home at 9 Greenleaf Drive responding to the second alarm, I could see the glow of the fire from my front door. Once there, I observed that the forward part of the tank and the tractor were completely involved in flame. As the off-loading area is in a narrow alley between the cement walls of a dike and the boiler room, water could only be applied from the front or rear of the vehicle. I immediately struck a general alarm. This brought in mutual aid from Middleton, Peabody, Beverly, Salem, Wenham, Lynn, Marblehead, Lynnfield, Hamilton, Ipswich, North Reading, Topsfield, and a foam truck from Logan Airport. Andover covered at our central station.

The flames from the tractor kept impinging upon the tank, causing the safety valves to release excessive built-up pressure. Keep in mind that this inferno was in the middle of a very expansive chemical complex. Surrounding the fire were dozens of containers of hydrogen and sodium, two highly active and explosive elements. The initial explosion also ruptured the main oil line feeding the plant's boiler, thus releasing thousands of gallons of warm bunker "C" fuel. This added to the treacherous conditions underfoot along with ten inches of snow.

We attempted on several occasions to close the valves that control the flow of the propane, but to no avail. As the fire increased in intensity, the release of pressure in the tank caused a very eerie sound. When the tires on the tractor blew out one by one, every firefighter's heart stopped for a few seconds.

I was at the rear of the building handling the situation in that area, and Deputy Wessell was doing the same thing in the front. I was standing near a deck gun manned by several Salem men when the first tire blew. Several of those firefighters tried to run but fell to the ground slipping on the heavy, murky oil coating the yard. After they had returned to their position, I told them with a chuckle that if it had been the tank that had let go, there would be no need to run.

After about an hour and a half into the fire fight and after having closed all the valves that should have stopped the flow of gas, we determined that the controls must have been damaged in the initial explosion. There is what is referred to as a "king" valve located at the bottom of the tank that directly controls the gas flow as it leaves the tank. To close this valve required the raw courage of two exceptionally brave firefighters. Under the protection of several water streams, Lieutenant Robert Flachbart and Firefighter Ronald Skinner advanced nearly halfway down under the belly of the tank and with great difficulty closed that valve.

Chief Leland Martin presents Lieutenant Robert Flachbart and Firefighter Ronald Skinner commendations for their brave actions during the Ventron fire, which actions prevented a potential catastrophe.

Their action succeeded in stopping the escape of propane. The half dozen deck guns and twice as many hand lines that were delivering water to the sides of the tank prevented it from reaching a pressure that would cause it to rupture. About a half hour after the king valve was closed, the fire was finally extinguished. Now started the grim task of picking up our equipment thoroughly covered with tar-like oil. The hose lines were worthless and left at the fire scene. A little later the Ventron Corporation replaced almost $20,000 worth of hose.

There were nearly one hundred firefighters actively engaged in this conflagration. If the tank had exploded, I honestly believe everyone of us would have been a fatality, and this account would not have been written.

The following is a letter of commendation that I wrote to the members of the Danvers Fire Department and signed by Town Manager Wayne Marquis and me:

Please excuse the delay in posting this communication, but there have been a lot of thoughts going through my mind and I did not want to do this in haste.

The late night and early morning of February 14, and 15 will long be remembered by most of us. We all experienced a point in our lives that could have been very dramatic to say nothing of everlasting. To all of you who participated in any way, I extend to you the highest of commendations for the unlimited courage and dedication exhibited.

There are seldom opportunities in our lives when such imminent danger is before us and everyone of you stood your ground and were an extreme credit to your profession. Hopefully we will never have to repeat this experience again.

I would like to make a special commendation to the courage and unflinching actions taken by Danvers firefighters Lt. Robert Flachbart and Firefighter Ronald Skinner who went in under the tank to shut off the flow of liquid and vapor. This action permitted the control and extinguishment of the fire.

To one and all, I want to thank you again for your exemplary courage and dedication—A JOB WELL DONE!

In March of 1984, *Firehouse Magazine*, a nationwide trade publication of the fire service, presented Robert Flachbart and Ronald Skinner with its heroism and community service award for their valiant actions at the Ventron fire.

Two other events of 1983 were the replacing of all our air masks with Scott air packs and twenty extra bottles or cylinders of compressed air and putting into service a new chief's car at a cost of $8,000.

On May 16, a very devastating fire struck downtown Peabody. Commonly referred to as the Henry Leather Fire, it not only involved the Henry leather complex, but a half dozen other large buildings as well. Those of us from Danvers worked with an engine and a ladder company on Howley Street. We were successful there in preventing the fire from jumping this road. Deputy Wessell and his crew drafted water from a nearby brook and supplied our lines to other apparatus working on the fire lines. Several of our firefighters were treated and released from the Hunt Hospital for the inhalation of toxic smoke: Richard Chase, Richard Osgood, David Sullivan, James McPherson, Robert Cyr, and I.

In 1985, our fire prevention program had been improved, and every year, under the guidance of Deputy Wessell and Fire Prevention Officer Lieutenant Michael Skinner, other improvements were made. To assist children of the community, the Danvers Rotary Club donated to the fire department "Pluggy," a battery-operated robot fire hydrant that walks and talks and rolls its eyes. It is a very useful tool and certainly gets the attention of young people.

On May 23 at 8:29 a.m., this department, after nearly three years of effort and much opposition, installed a new communications system. Agitation for it had actually started several years before because of the action of sunspots on our radio transmission. Instead of radio waves going up and then directly down, as a result of this phenomenon, they would ascend into the ionosphere, and then travel horizontally for thousands of miles before being picked up by other receivers on our frequency. Naturally it caused extreme annoyance and interference, often at critical times.

This new center is located in a specially designed room in the police station. It is arranged so that three operating positions can be utilized during serious conditions, but under normal situations only two are: one for the fire dispatcher and the other for the police dispatcher. All alarms and other means of communication are received there and then retransmitted. Our radio frequency is now 483.3375 with our main antenna located on the water tower of the Danvers State Hospital with its elevation of three hundred twenty-seven feet. There are also three repeaters, devices that receive electronic communication signals and deliver corresponding amplified ones. Our mobile radios have a range of twenty miles and our portable ones, up to ten miles.

When this center went into operation, it relieved our needs for a desk man at headquarters since all dispatchers are civilians. With him now back on the apparatus, it improved each group by one additional active firefighter.

Continuing this year, as they have done every Labor Day weekend since 1981, the Danvers Firefighters Union, Local 2038, held its annual drive for Muscular Dystrophy. Firefighters choose strategic locations on routes where there are stop lights. When traffic comes to a halt, they go from car to car with a fireman's boot to collect donations for Jerry's Kids, named for the comedian Jerry Lewis who emcees this drive's national telethon. I don't enjoy doing this, but it is for a very commendable cause. Up through 1985, we had collected $56,255. Four years later the total was $118,539.

In March of 1986, we placed a new pump into service. It is another Emergency One 1250 g.p.m. pump with automatic transmission and a five hundred gallon booster tank. Its body work is all aluminum construction. This custom-made vehicle cost $128,120.

This year also saw us entering the computer age. Installed in the chief's office was a Digital terminal from the town's main frame computer. With such a versatile tool, we are able to record all instances of fire and other activities of the department. Every bit of this vital information is now ready at our beck and call and will be a great asset to our overall operations. A camcorder, which will greatly aid in our training exercises and to document fire hazards and various fires, was also purchased.

Throughout 1987 the incidence of fire was neither good nor bad. Even though we had over twenty-five hundred responses, there were no fires of dramatic importance. However, because it was a very dry spring, we had an unusual number of woods and grass fires. Our inspection program was modified. All industrial and commercial buildings within Danvers were to be inspected by each group at least semi-annually. Violation forms were initiated and within a reasonable period of time, any violations were to be followed by reinspection. Finally the cab of our Engine 3 was completely renovated by Greenwood Fire Apparatus Company of North Attleboro for $3,270.

Our Ladder 1, which was delivered February of 1969, had its tractor replaced in 1983 with a Maxim-made one. Maxim, now a part of Seagrave, had the North American rights to the German Magirus metal aerial ladder which was rear mounted, creating a smaller, more maneuverable rig than the older, longer aerial ladder trucks.

The Henry Leather fire in Peabody on May 16, 1983.

We had the trailer refurbished by E. J. Murphy Company for the sum of $24,994. At the annual town meeting, $65,000 was appropriated for this work, leaving us with a balance of $40,006. Our Ladder 2, a 1947, sixty-five foot Pirsch aerial, which had been purchased for the sum of $16,500, was sold to collector David Towle of Brookfield, New Hampshire, for the sum of $2,610. It had served the department well.

At the time we were negotiating the sale of our Ladder 2, Beverly was in the process of purchasing a new ladder truck from Greenwood. However, it had run over its budget for the new aerial by $20,000. To overcome this deficit, the city traded its old Ladder 1 for $20,000. We needed a reserve ladder truck, so I negotiated with the company to purchase Beverly's Ladder for that sum, using the $40,006 balance. Our mechanic, Arnold Weeks, did a lot of refurbishing and brought it up to good working condition. It is now our reserve Ladder 2.

Additional purchases that year included a new jaws of life device to free victims trapped inside motor vehicles or other confined spaces. Our former jaws of life was reconditioned, so that we have one of these on both ladder companies. We also bought an additional one-thousand feet of 4" supply hose. All of our engine companies now have a minimum of nine hundred feet of this hose in a divided hose bed or compartment with 2 1/2" and 3" hose in the other bed.

At 12:49 a.m. on April 16, 1988, fire alarm dispatch center received a call that the smoke alarm at 10 Charles Street had been activated. Upon arrival of the first engine company, we found heavy fire issuing from a room on the second floor front. There was then a second alarm sounded. The fire was of suspicious origin from the beginning. After a very lengthy and comprehensive investigation, the accused arsonist was convicted following a four-day jury trial and spent five years in Cedar Junction (Walpole State Prison).

Captain Robert Cyr, who played a very vital role in this case, worked closely with the state police from the fire marshal's office. His testimony at the trial was very critical in obtaining a conviction. Arson is the hardest crime to get a guilty verdict. Seldom do arson cases go to trial because there might have been an accidental cause for the fire.

On July 17, 1989, we purchased an Emergency One Hush Pump for the sum of $165,000. This has a completely enclosed four-door, six-man cab with the engine in the rear. The cab is so arranged that all the men can have their air packs on as the backseat rest is designed so that the air bottles fit into recesses. The vehicle is equipped with a 1250 g.p.m. single-stage pump and a five hundred gallon booster tank with two crosslay skid hose loads to permit dropping working lines at a fire. This apparatus is quite unusual and the first of its type on the North Shore.

It became available through a unique process. The distributor for Emergency One, Greenwood Motors of North Attleboro, did not have a vehicle to show at the New England Fire Chiefs' Association Conference. So it ordered this vehicle from Emergency One and paid for it themselves in order that they would have something to exhibit. After about three months of paying $1,500 per month interest to Emergency One, Greenwood decided it would be financially wise to seek an interested buyer.

I had been an acquaintance of the owner of the company for more than twenty-five years and fortunately for the town, he thought of me first. The arrangement was that he would make minor modifications to suit our needs and then sell it to us at his exact cost, but we had to do it before his next payment was due at the bank. Because the town has a capital account where money is put into it at the annual town meeting, the money was readily available. By buying this apparatus one year ahead of schedule and under these conditions, the town saved more than $25,000.

There were also other changes in vehicles. We purchased a chief's car, a new Ford, for $12,570. A new one-ton, four-wheel pickup truck was acquired for $15,975 to replace Squad 1. We sold our American LaFrance Engine 4 to David Towle, the collector from New Hampshire, for the sum of $575.00. Danvers Motor Company once more loaned us a new car for the use of the deputy.

On June 15, 1989, Ventron experienced another disastrous fire. This one occurred in a corrugated metal building 75' x 100'. Sodium hydride was being transferred from one container to another. A flexible rubber hose was used for the purpose. Unfortunately the pressure and the heat of the sodium was not compatible with the rubber in the hose. It caused the hose to rupture, allowing the sodium to flow onto the ground where it ignited on contact with the moist air. The smoke given off by this fire could be seen for many miles as it was a bril-

Chief Martin directs operations at a fire at the Danvers Paper Company, the former Creese & Cook Building, on September 23, 1985.

liant white against a deep blue sky. The sodium eventually burned for more than an hour. Dozens of explosions shook the main building and the surrounding ones. Here again, Ventron's employees assisted us greatly.

An interesting incident occurred during this fire fight. I was standing beside a deck gun that was delivering approximately five-hundred gallons of water per minute when the direction of the nozzle was changed, and I was hit square in the chest by the stream. It threw me a distance of about twenty feet. I turned over once in the air.

Very fortunately, the only injury I sustained was to my ego. I picked myself up and went back directing the operation. Once the men realized that I was not hurt, they thought it was one real funny act I had put on. It certainly brightened their day. (By the way, I have known several firefighters who have been seriously injured in this same manner. There is an ex-Beverly fireman who was so severely injured that he had to retire.)

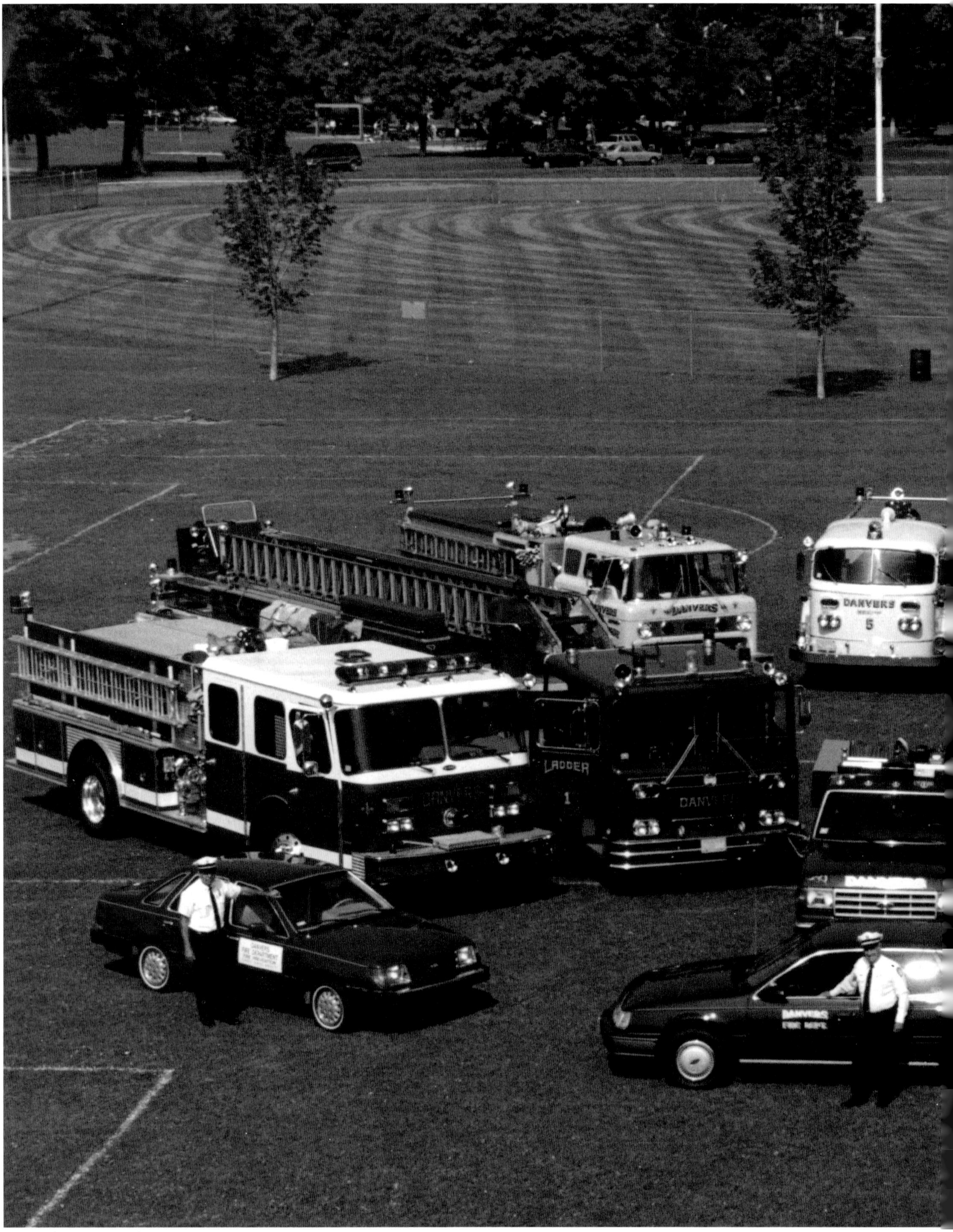
DANVERS
5
LADDER
1
DANVERS

From left Deputy Chief Richard Wessell, Chief Martin and Lieutenant Michael Skinner stand in front of the Danvers Fire Department vehicles in this 1989 aerial view taken at Plains Park.

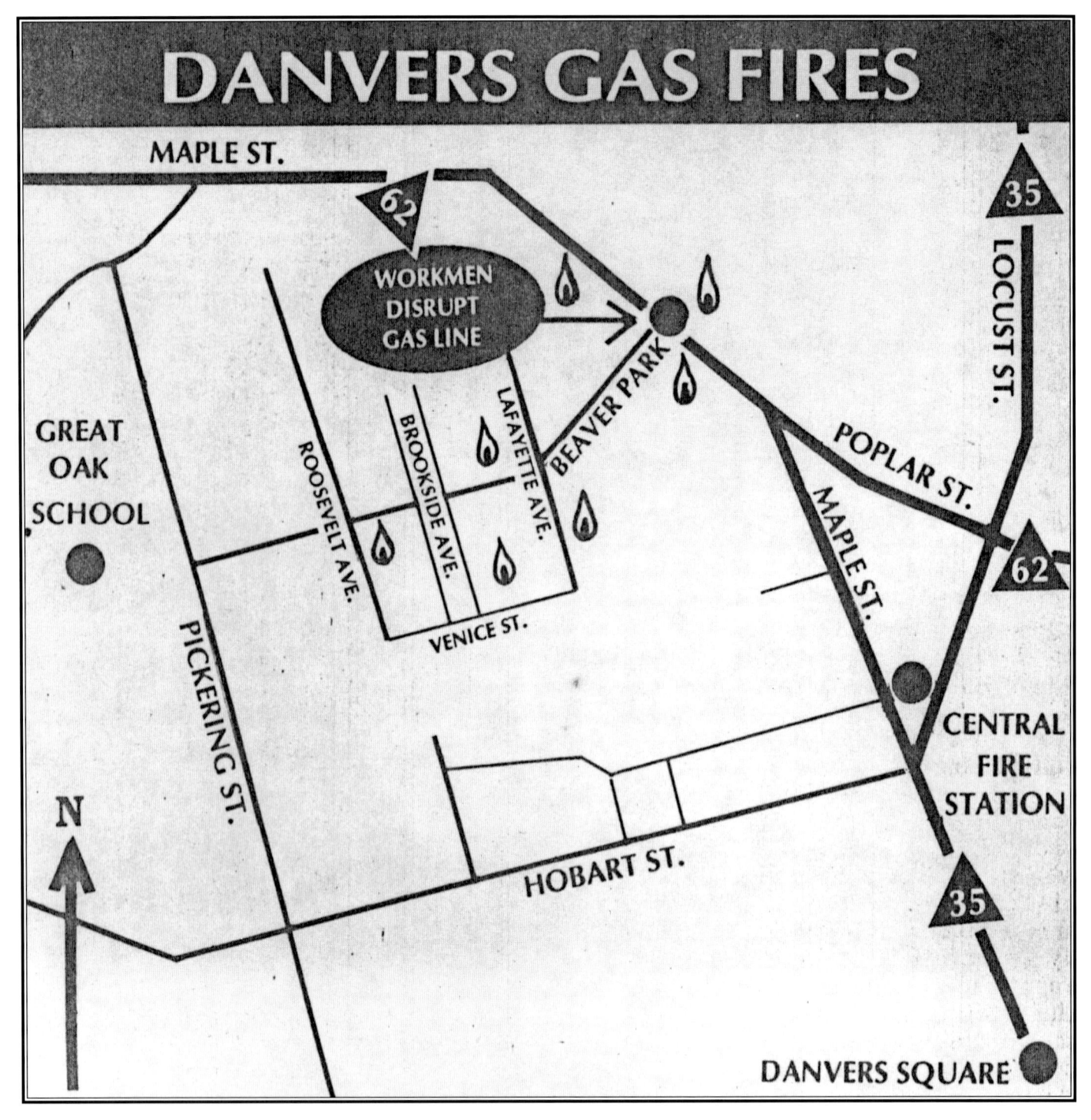

This map reproduced in the **Danvers Herald** *indicated the locations of the major gas fires on April 2, 1990.*

CHAPTER X

Beaver Park Catastrophe

Sometimes one catastrophe follows another, leaving firefighters exhausted physically and emotionally. During the late fall and early winter of 1989, we were busy with several serious house fires caused in part by an extremely cold December. Then in the spring of 1990 we became even busier. On March 6 at approximately 3:41 a.m., the fire alarm dispatch center received a call that the house at 26 Delaware Avenue was on fire. At the same time, police officer Dana Hagan, on routine patrol, reported that he was going to investigate the reason for a red glow above the area where he was.

A few minutes later Engine 1, the first company to be dispatched, said that when they were at the intersection of Summer Street and Labao Drive, they could actually see tongues of flames licking the night sky. Captain Arnold Cyr ordered both a second alarm and Engine 3 to the scene, a two and a half story house with a two-car garage beneath. The roof had already collapsed into the second floor which, in turn, had fallen into the first floor and the basement.

In my forty-four years on the department, I never saw a dwelling so fully consumed upon the arrival of the first company. Unfortunately, the two occupants of the home died in the fire. One body was found in the first floor living room and the other, in the basement. This is only the second dual fatality we have experienced in the history of the Danvers Fire Department. The other was in that airplane crash on Massachusetts Avenue.

Earlier in this history, I described several major Danvers fires like those at the Fossa Block and Max Berry's woodworking shop on School Street. Now I shall attempt to relate the epic of what I believe to be our most serious Danvers fire.

On Monday, April 2, 1990, Group 4 was on duty. Captain Robert Cyr was the officer in charge. It was cloudy, a light drizzle was falling, and the temperature at 8:00 a.m. was forty-nine degrees. The wind was blowing at five miles from the west. It seemed a routine day. Workmen at the Hardcover Restaurant on Route 1 north-bound had accidently set off Box 2182. After lunch, a smoke drill was conducted at headquarters because we had just acquired a new positive pressure fan that was very effective in removing smoke from a building.

After that, the headquarters group went to the second floor to have coffee. Then Engine 2, Lieutenant James McPherson in charge, left the central station, proceeded up Locust Street and was going to put Box 2183 at the Ferncroft Business Building back in service. Engine 3 with Lieutenant David Price in command, returned to their quarters.

A fatal house fire occurred at 26 Delaware Avenue the early morning of March 6, 1990.

While all this was transpiring, approximately eight Boston Gas Company employees were testing the new regulator installed on Maple Street at the intersection of Beaver Brook Road, a crossroads which shall be referred to hereafter as Point Zero. Inadvertently one of the men opened the valve from the high pressure gas main allowing the gas, still under pressure, to surge into the low pressure, smaller gas main by way of the series of by-pass piping. What had been done by the compay to provide customers with improved service during peak periods turned into a disaster in a matter of six minutes, 3:12 to 3:18 p.m.

The pilots in many home gas appliances suddenly increased from their normal one half inch to as high as several feet. In many instances, this caused the flame to set fire to wooden kitchen cabinets. In at least two cases where gas heaters were involved, combustibles near them resulted in cellar fires.

Most of the ensuing incidents occurred within a quarter mile radius of the regulator. But there were exceptions. Though more than a mile away, Burroughs Street was affected. A resident there, who was boiling potatoes, reported that the flames coming from her range increased to a point eighteen inches above the pot she was using. This same type of happening was observed even farther away on Elliott, Locust, and Lawrence Streets.

Maple Street is a highly traveled route, and the neighborhood at the junction of Maple and Beaver Park Road, i.e. Point Zero, is fairly congested with single

Smoke bellows from the rear and side of the home at 6 Beaver Park Road.

and two-family dwellings. The road descends at a very sharp angle into Beaver Park, which has mainly single-family residences except for two condominium complexes.

Seven structures within this area with a real estate value of $5,845,100 were seriously impacted by the fire. No estimate of the value of the destroyed contents in these dwellings was ever given. Three of the seven structures required a one-alarm response. Two needed a two-alarm response, and the two condominiums had to have a three-alarm assistance. I recall that there were at least twenty other fires and several gas leaks controlled by the homeowners themselves, the police department, or other fire departments, but we have no written records of these. Keep in mind that all these fires happened within six minutes. Let's now take a closer look at them.

At 3:12 p.m., the fire alarm center received the first of dozens of calls. Engine 1 and Ladder 1 were sent to 15 Lafayette Street for a house fire. Engine 3 was also dispatched to that address. En route the captain received several radio reports of numerous other fires and explosions. Engine 2 while proceeding up Locust Street heard the messages to Engine 1. The driver turned around in Donegal Circle and drove toward Beaver Park Road informing fire alarm of his action.

Engine 3 and Squad 1 respond to fight the house fire at 11 Beaver Park Road.

Meanwhile Engine 1 was approaching their destination. The Boston Gas Company work party pointed to the home of Dorothy Kowalski at 6 Beaver Park Road. When they stopped there, Captain Robert Cyr was told by off-duty firefighter Ronald Skinner that a woman was trapped on the second floor.

Skinner and Firefighter Bill Trefrey carried a 1 3/4" hose to the front door, but due to the intensity of the fire the advance was halted. Ladder 1 pulled up behind Engine 1, and Firefighter Fred Ingraham and Lieutenant Michael Skinner took a sixteen-foot ground ladder from Ladder 1 and carried it into the driveway. They threw it up to the second floor, second window in on the driveway side. Heavy flames and smoke were showing here at the ceiling level. Ingraham climbed the ladder and called to Mrs. Kowalski to come to him. The intense heat and flame literally forced her headfirst out the window and into Ingraham's arms. On the ground the victim was found to have severe burns around both ankles, so Firefighter George Snow played the stream from the 1 3/4" line over her legs. She was then removed to Hunt Memorial Hospital on Lindall Hill via Lyons Ambulance Service.

Engine 1 had advanced a second 1 3/4" line to the rear hall and entryway where the men were confronted by a sheet of flame. Under very difficult and hazardous conditions, they got the hose farther into the hallway towards the kitchen stove where the main body of fire was situated. After it was knocked down, the line was then advanced up the rear stairway to the second floor where it extinguished this second fire. It was rumored (as is often the case under such circumstances) that another woman was in the house. Captain Cyr and Lieutenant McPherson entered through the front door despite the danger and made a thorough search in all rooms, closets, and under beds. They ascertained that there was no other person in the house.

When Engine 3 had arrived here and Lieutenant David Price was alighting from the cab, he was confronted by Christopher Crowley, who informed him that his home was on fire. Looking down the road in the direction that the young man was pointing, Price saw heavy flames and smoke coming from the rear of 11 Beaver Park Road. He yelled to Captain Cyr and received permission to take his apparatus there. The men laid a four inch supply line into their own pump to draw water from their tank. Firefighters Ronnie Moreland, Ronald Skinner, Dick Kennedy, and Lieutenant Price advanced a 1 3/4" line into the cellar by way of the rear bulkhead. As the heat in the basement was intense, it made conditions very difficult. There was already extensive damage in the cellar and kitchen area. The walls and ceilings in the kitchen and on the second floor above it had to be overhauled, i.e., opened up and checked for any extension of the fire.

I was at the Hunt Nursing Home across from the Hunt Hospital when I heard the first report on my portable radio. When I got to the scene a few minutes later, fire alarm dispatch told me that they were getting calls of several other fires in the immediate vicinity. How I do not know, but it then occurred to me that the only reason there could be several fires in these different buildings was that there must be a connection between them and the gas company crew working on Maple Street. Leaving Deputy Chief Dick Wessell and Captain Bob Cyr in charge of the fire at 6 Beaver Park Road, I drove back to Point Zero to confront the gas company men. As I got our of my car, Engine 2 approached me coming up Maple. I directed them to go down and assist Engine 1. I then called fire alarm to transmit a second alarm, the time now being 3:18 p.m. I also requested Beverly to cover and Middleton to come to the fire scene.

When I was free of these duties, I went over to the men and asked them if they had any knowledge of what the cause might be. They all looked at me with blank expressions. Not one person offered any information. At this time, fire alarm communicated to me that both Beverly and Middleton were responding and also that they were receiving several more calls for fires in this general area. Once again I asked the men if they knew the cause of the fires. This second request was made in a rather loud tone. I said, "What in the hell are you guys doing?" Sheepishly, one of them told me. They assured me that the valves had been closed, and everything was back to normal.

I now received a call from fire alarm that smoke was coming from the house at 192 Maple located only about one hundred feet from where I was standing. I looked and saw a heavy concentration of smoke billowing up from the basement windows of this two and a half story house with its three apartments. Things happened quickly in the next few minutes.

I called fire alarm and requested them to again call Middleton and urge them politely to quickly respond to the fire. As I approached 192 Maple, a woman from 195 Maple came up to me screaming that her house was on fire. I asked if everyone was out of the dwelling. After being told that no one was inside, I entered the rear door of 192 to be sure that no one was inside there. I had proceeded half way across the kitchen before I was driven back by the flames coming up from the basement. I got out of there and again called fire alarm to find out where in the hell Middleton was. I also requested that the Beverly pump, their Engine 6, come directly to the fire and for Salem to cover headquarters. Also that Wenham and Topsfield come directly to the fire. I gave these orders

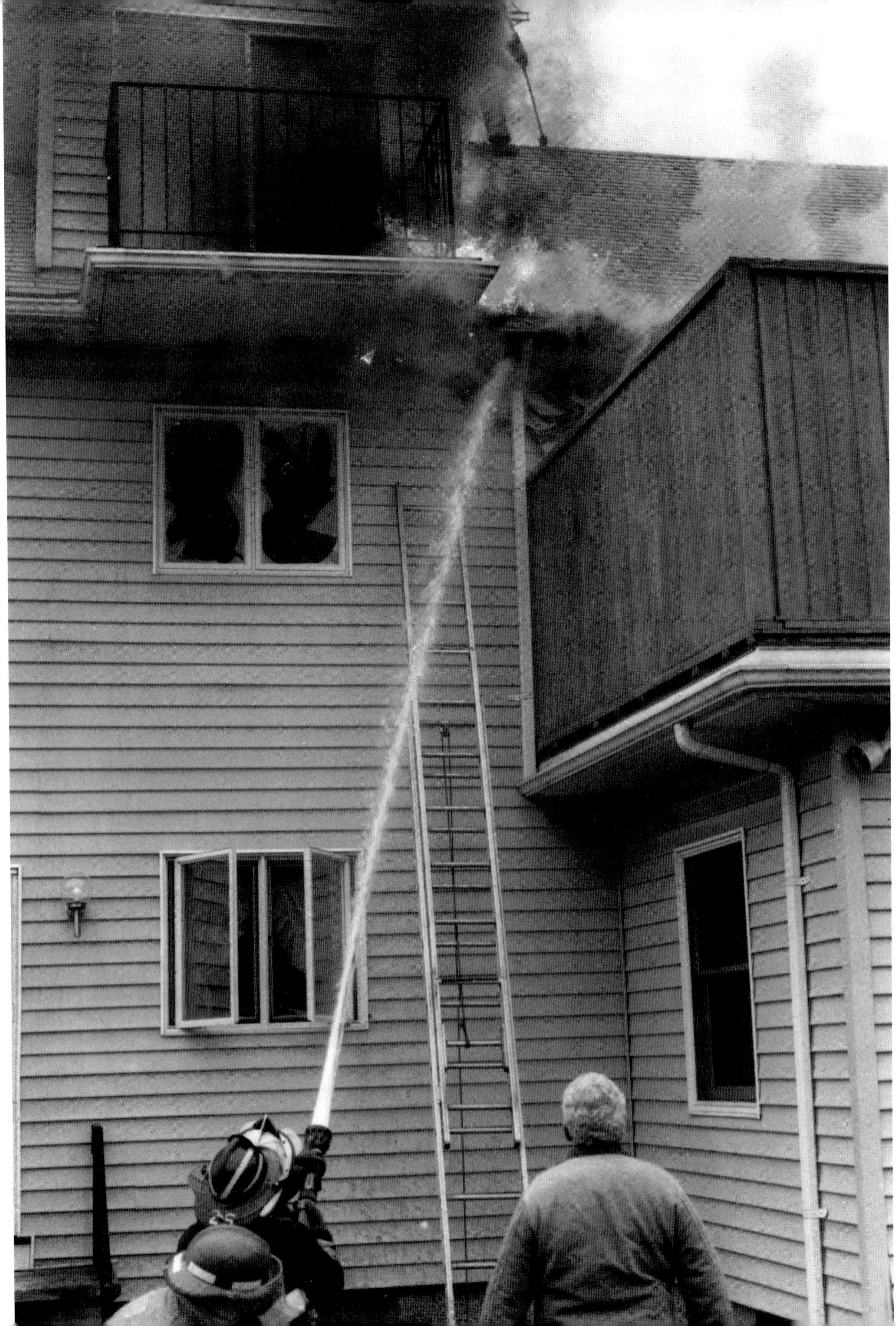

while walking back to Point Zero. The woman from 195 Maple, at least I think it was her, kept yelling at me that her house was on fire and what was I going to do about it. Then another woman met me, crying that her house was full of gas and was going to blow up.

At 3:22 p.m. I received information from fire alarm that the condominium at 15 Lafayette Avenue was reporting several apartments on fire. I ordered a third alarm and told the alarm center to go to Phase II and have Beverly control handle all county fire communications from this time on. I further ordered our fire alarm to tell Beverly's fire alarm to send twelve more mutual-aid engine companies directly to the fire, and I would meet them at Point Zero and direct them from there. I was then informed that several fires were being reported from the condominium at 6 Venice Street.

As I stood there in the middle of Maple Street, a peculiar feeling came over me that this could be the beginning of the biggest experience of my career. Looking over the scene from my vantage point, I could see pillars of smoke rising from a half dozen or more fires. Everyone that had a radio transmitter was pleading for more assistance and apparatus. Hearing the fever pitch of their voices, I knew that Mrs. Martin's little boy had better remain calm, think clearly, and recall all the hard lessons drilled into me by John Clougherty.

My thoughts were abruptly interrupted by the welcome arrival of Middleton's Engine 1 with Captain Henry Michalski, Jr., Lieutenant George Kimball, and Firefighters Timothy O'Connell and Frank Twiss aboard. They laid a four-inch line from a hydrant at 197 Maple Street and advanced their vehicle to the front of 192 Maple. To me it had felt like hours before this first mutual-aid apparatus arrived.

It must have seemed that way to Deputy Wessell also. Located at the intersection of Beaver Park Road and Lafayette Street, he was vigorously requesting that equipment and manpower be sent to him. Since I was situated such that responding apparatus had to meet me first, I had the opportunity of assigning them to the various fires. I promptly dispatched the first arriving companies to my two fires on Maple Street. Soon after Middleton arrived, Danvers Engine 5 appeared and took up a position in front of 195 Maple with off-duty Lieutenant Richard Chase as officer in charge.

Now I had to turn my attention to the condominium at 6 Venice, a three-story wood frame with brick veneer, thirty-six unit apartment house. I asked Chief Kenneth Pelonzi with Beverly Engine 6, who now approached me from the Danvers Square side of the fire, to proceed to this building where he would be directed by Deputy Wessell.

Upon arrival there, Chief Pelonzi saw smoke and fire showing from apartment C4 on the second floor and heavy black smoke coming from apartments E1 and E2 on the lower level. He was informed by off-duty Deputy Chief John DeAngelo of the Peabody Fire Department that the building had been evacuated. The Beverly men then laid two hundred feet of hose as a feeder or supply line into their pump. They vented two windows on the second floor using ground ladders and got a 1 3/4" handline through the front door.

Advancing under extreme smoke conditions to the second floor, they knocked down the fire in apartment C4. Please make special note that due to the

Facing page: Firefighters play their hose on the three family apartment at 192 Maple Street.

severity of the conditions, manpower was desperately short and even the chief of the Beverly Fire Department put on an airpack and led his men in combatting this very serious blaze. In the meantime, John De Angelo, using his own radio, called both Peabody and Beverly control and requested two additional pumps and a ladder to help at the Venice Street emergency.

The multi-unit Fairlane Condominium complex located at 6 Venice Street had several fires break out simultaneously.

I was in contact with Beverly fire alarm by way of my car telephone since there was so much conversation on our radio frequency. Beverly control informed me that we would soon have the requested twelve more engine companies and three more ladder companies as well. They asked where staging areas should be set up after sufficient fireground apparatus had arrived. I determined one staging area would be at the Danvers Plaza. The other would be in the parking lot across from the Central Fire Station. These areas eventually held one ladder and three engine companies apiece. However, this reserve force was assembled only after fireground needs had been met.

When an Ipswich engine company appeared, I directed it to aid Beverly's Engine 6 at 6 Venice. Upon the men's arrival there, they advanced lines to apartments E1 and E2 and extinguished kitchen fires in each unit. I called our fire alarm and asked that the next arriving ladder company, which was from North Reading, go to the same address. To permit the escape of smoke and heated air, this second company and another from Saugus that followed right after them vented the roof. All the combined ladder and engine companies worked in concert with Chief Pelonzi directing the over-all fire fighting. They found smaller fires in apartments B2 and B4. Complete and thorough overhauling as well as ventilation was conducted by all these fire crews.

Shortly after striking the second alarm, I had requested fire control to have Wenham and Topsfield come directly to the fire command post at Point Zero. At approximately 3:26 p.m., just fourteen minutes after the start of this catastrophe, Topsfield's engine company appeared. I asked that they lay supply lines from the hydrant at the corner of Maple and Summer Streets into Danvers Engine 5 at 195 Maple. Equipped with masks, this crew advanced the 1 3/4" line to the second floor to cut off the upward extension of fire. In the meantime, Lieutenant Richard Chase, who had driven Danvers Engine 4 to the fire, ordered a Middleton crew to advance another line into the basement there where they encountered heavy smoke and a fire between the floor joists above the hot water heater. Lynnfield Engine 1 also laid a supply line into Engine 5's tank and then advanced an attack line into the first floor and checked the hot walls in the kitchen around the chimney breast. These walls were opened, and the spread of the fire was stopped.

The fire at this address was confined to the basement and the first floor kitchen area with very heavy smoke conditions throughout the remainder of the two and a half story structure. The gas main was shut off, and two Topsfield firefighters remained here for overhaul.

Immediately following Topsfield to the fire scene, Wenham's engine company arrived. I ordered them to report to Deputy Wessell, who subsequently directed them to the Park Lane Condominiums at 15 Lafayette. There they reported to Lieutenant Michael Skinner, who ordered them to position their pump in the parking lot in front of the building. A Peabody engine company then appeared, and I told them also to go to 15 Lafayette, where Deputy Wessell had this engine lay a supply line into the Wenham pumper.

My attention was next turned to the fire at 192 Maple, which now had ascended to the second floor. At this particular time, the situation became very difficult to coordinate because Deputy Wessell needed even more engine companies for the condominium fires at the Park Lane. I looked to the right at 192 Maple and observed that the fire had spread to all floors and only the Middleton crew was valiantly attacking it. At this time, two other companies luckily arrived simultaneously from Swampscott and Manchester-by-the-Sea.

I yielded to the pleas of my deputy and dispatched both these new engines to his assistance. Swampscott attacked the fire at 15 Lafayette advancing up the southern stairshaft. The Peabody and the Wenham crews advanced into the center door, and the Manchester men advanced lines up the north stairshaft. Again, as at 6 Venice, heavy fire conditions were encountered in several apartments making advancement very difficult. Danvers Ladder 1 was operating here and soon performed some admirable ventilation work. Being successful in this regard means not only in the direction they wanted the heat to escape but also in making a chimney effect for the products of combustion to exit.

At approximately 3:30 p.m. Salem's Engine 1 was called to the fire from headquarters. I now knew that I had no apparatus in reserve in a staging area and again called Beverly control by telephone and urged them to speed up the dispatch of those promised apparatus since fire alarm was still receiving calls. With the Salem pump on the scene, I had that crew lay a line from the hydrant directly behind my position and then lay another supply line into Middleton's pump in front of 192 Maple. I saw another pump approaching up Maple and a woman

Fire companies from Salem, Marblehead and Middleton assist in the attacking of the fire at 192 Maple Street.

running out into the street frantically waving her arms. The pump abruptly stopped; then I observed those men running a preconnected line into the house at 168 Maple.

Middleton's Ladder 1 now came onto the scene. I ordered that crew to throw their stick (ladder) to the roof of 192 Maple and ventilate that residence. Again, looking down Maple towards the Square, I saw another beautiful pump nearing. It was Marblehead's Engine 1 with Chief Charles Maurais. When it stopped at the command post, I asked him to take his crew and advance lines into 192 Maple also and as the senior officer there to take charge.

Middleton had already advanced a 1 3/4" line through the front door. Chief Maurais had another line advanced through the rear door. He next ordered two additional lines to be advanced into the second floor. The men on these lines were taking a terrific beating since the fire had gained considerable headway because of the delay of arriving apparatus.

When North Reading and North Andover engines appeared, I assigned their manpower also to Chief Maurais. A North Andover firefighter, while working on the third floor, became exhausted and had to be removed to the Hunt Hospital by Lyons Ambulance Service. Lieutenant Chase, after supervising the knockdown of the fire at 195 Maple, came across the street to the one at 192 Maple. He was soon actively engaged in fighting his second fire of the afternoon.

When I again looked down Maple Street, I saw Essex Engine 1 approaching.

Originally assigned to cover at headquarters, it had been diverted to me. Just as the pump was nearing 189 Maple, another homeowner beckoned to these men by frantically waving his arms. They discovered that his house was fully charged with escaping gas, so they forced the cellar door, donned masks, entered the premises, and turned off the meter. After carefully ventilating that residence, they reported to me. I ordered them to proceed to 192 Maple.

The crew from Lynnfield now appeared on the scene at approximately 3:35 p.m. It was Engine 4 with Chief Paul Romano. They laid a three-inch line into Engine 5 of Danvers. While the chief's crew was doing this, Lieutenant Chase came out of 195 Maple and asked him for help in charging his line. Chief Romano engaged the pump and filled the line with water ready for use and under pressure from Engine 5 while Deputy Francis Lennon, Lieutenant Steven Allison, and Firefighter Ann Topping donned masks and assisted in the attack on that dwelling before moving on to the next fire at 200 Maple, where a cellar fire had been reported in progress. After checking the residence and finding no fire, they reported to Chief Maurais, who requested that the Lynnfield crew help in the interior attack on 192 Maple as many of the men at the fire were becoming severely exhausted. Meanwhile, Lieutenant Chase, who was actively engaged in fire fighting on the third floor, became disoriented and had to be led out to the street, whereupon a Lyons ambulance took him to the Hunt. He was treated there for exhaustion and later released.

It was at this time that Deputy Wessell had ordered Lieutenant Skinner to the Park Lane Condominiums at 15 Lafayette, where there were reports of several fires. Skinner sized up the situation there and requested another engine and a ladder company. I was still at the command post at Point Zero when Peabody's Engine 1 had stopped for my orders. I sent them, you will recall, to Deputy Wessell, who told them to lay a four-inch supply line to the front of the building, thereby allowing Peabody, with the help of Marblehead and Swampscott, to advance three 1 3/4" hand lines into units A and B, where there was heavy fire showing.

When Wenham's Engine 2 arrived with Chief Don Killam, he and his men attacked two fiercely burning fires in unit B. Also assisting in this overall operation at 15 Lafayette were Danvers Lieutenant McPherson and Firefighters David Sullivan, David DeLuca, Jim Brooks, David Morin, Richard Osgood, and Ford Smith. Every apartment in this complex was investigated for further extension of fire and then complete overhauling was done. Chief William Hyde of Swampscott also ably assisted Danvers, directing work primarily on the second floor in units C and D. Additional manpower was requested at this location and as Manchester's Engine 1 had just arrived, accompanied by their Chief Joseph O'Malley, I directed them to 15 Lafayette.

Now I received notification from our fire alarm that a very strong odor of gas had been reported from the Hunt Memorial Hospital, approximately a quarter of a mile from the Boston Gas Company's regulator pit where all the trouble had started in the first place.

As I got this news, a Gloucester engine company, along with their Chief Barry McKay, stopped and awaited my orders. I requested that they answer this latest call and report as soon as possible as to the situation there. Two gas crews also responded to the hospital call.

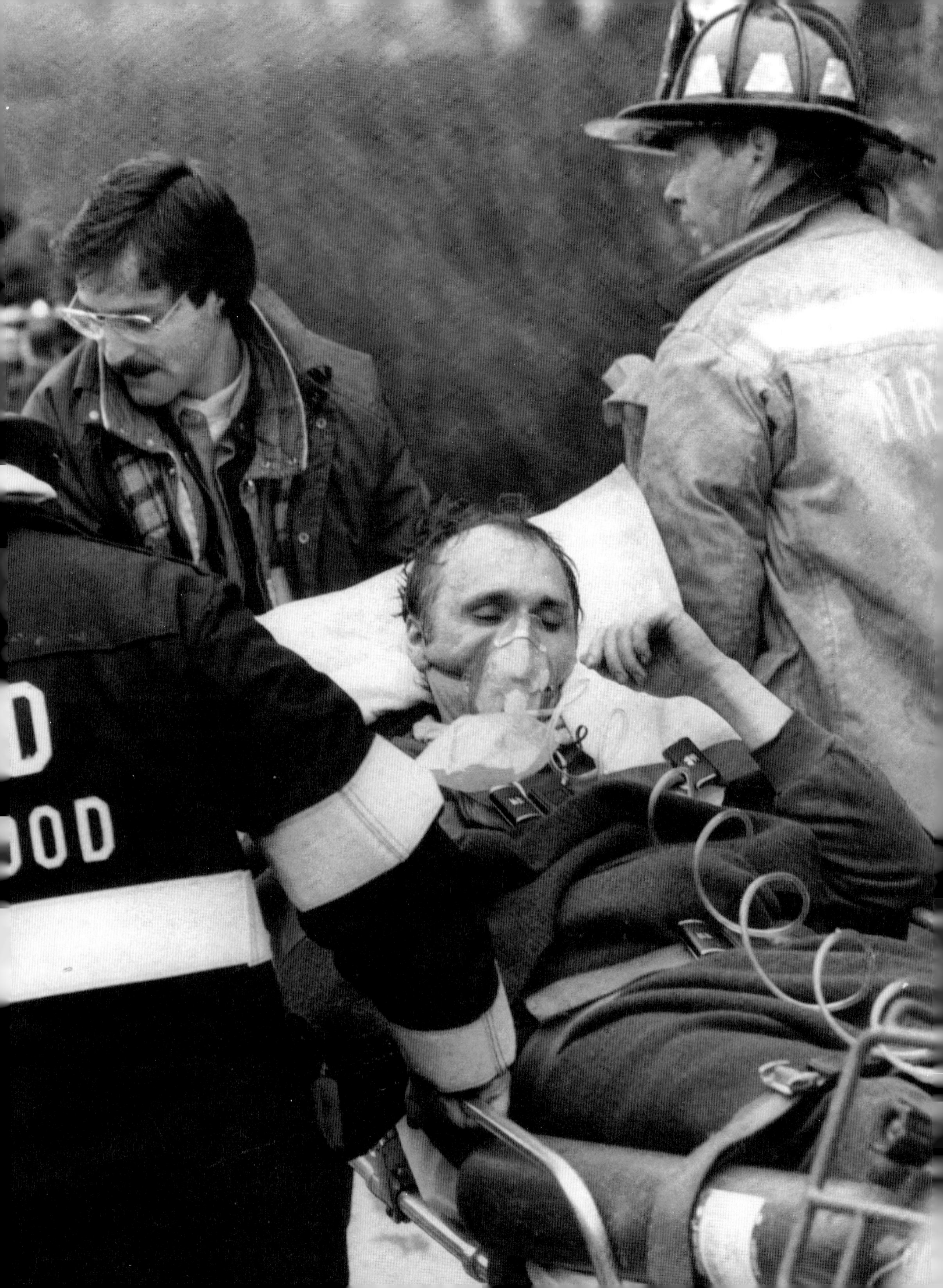

What these men found after they got to the Hunt was that when the high pressure gas had arrived there, it entered the building directly. As soon as the flow of gas reached the two meters, the pressure literally blew the metering mechanisms right out of their cases. This allowed the raw gas to flow with great rapidity into the telephone room. The smell quickly spread throughout the facility. Fortunately the maintenance people discovered the source of the problem and shut off the gas. Because of their prompt action, the hospital did not have to be evacuated.

At about 4:10 p.m., Hamilton's Ladder 1 came to our headquarters and was dispatched to 157 Maple Street to investigate the odor of gas. Lieutenant David Ellison and Firefighter Bryan Hill of that town, accompanied by a Danvers firefighter, opened the rear bulkhead door of this residence and confirmed the presence of gas. They evacuated eight people and vented the house. Assistant Chief Phillip Stevens of Hamilton also vented the house at 7 Poplar Street.

Hamilton's Ladder 1 then returned to our central station. At 4:30 p.m. Hamilton's cascade unit arrived at headquarters and started to refill depleted air bottles from its large oxygen tanks. Ten minutes later Ladder 1 was again dispatched, this time to 8 Winthrop Street. After that, it stayed at the junction of Winthrop and Lindall Streets to aid in blocking Winthrop. At the suggestion of the Danvers firefighter who was acting as their pilot, Firefighter Hill returned to headquarters with a portable radio which gave us contact with Wenham, Essex, and Ipswich as well as Hamilton. At approximately 5:30 p.m. a resident at 5 Hobart Street came to headquarters to report that his apartment had a very strong odor of gas. Salem's Engine 2 and Hamilton's Ladder 1 responded and discovered that the pilot lights were out and that is where the smell was coming from. Two second floor tenants had to be evacuated, and the dwelling was then thoroughly ventilated.

Lieutenant James McPherson with Firefighters Dick Kennedy and Fred Ingraham from our department was sent by Deputy Wessell to the Park Lane Condominiums at 15 Lafayette after the fire at 6 Beaver Park Road had been knocked down. There they were informed by a Peabody firefighter that David Sullivan was in the smoke-filled basement alone as he was the only man with air left except for Lieutenant McPherson, who soon entered the building to assist Sullivan. They knocked down one kitchen fire and then vented the apartment.

When McPherson ran out of air, he was relieved by Firefighter Brooks, who, along with Sullivan, performed extensive overhauling. There were several other apartments simultaneously on fire. Lieutenant Skinner ordered Ladder 1's crew to raise their stick to the roof in case the fire spread into the attic space.

When Malden's Rescue 2 cascade unit with one captain and four firefighters was sent to Deputy Wessell, he told them to take up a position between 6 Venice and 15 Lafayette and begin filling depleted air bottles. In total at this fire at 15 Lafayette were four engine companies, one ladder company, one attack unit, and the just-mentioned Malden Rescue. In terms of personnel, there were three chiefs, two deputy chiefs, three captains, three lieutenants, and twenty-three firefighters.

Facing page: Lieutenant Richard Chase receives oxygen and helping hands from fellow firefighters following his supervision of knocking down the fire at 195 Maple Street and assisting at 192 Maple Street.

One Swampscott firefighter was overcome and transported to Salem Hospital, where he was treated for smoke inhalation and then released. The Malden Rescue replenished a total of thirty-eight air bottles. Seven condominium units were gutted and left smoldering shells by the time all fires had been extinguished. Deputy Wessell, with the able assistance of Lieutenant Skinner, was responsible overall for the containment and extinuishment of this fire at 15 Lafayette.

Firefighter Robert Pyburn, who acted as a pilot for Rockport Engine 3, had been dispatched at about 3:35 p.m. from the staging area at headquarters to 158 Maple where a heavy odor of gas had been reported. The crew forced entry into the cellar and gas company men shut off the gas. They thoroughly and completely ventilated that building. From there, they were sent to a medical aid call at 13 Poplar; however, there was no medical problem, just another instance of gas seepage.

Firefighter Nicholas Serratore was the pilot of the Ipswich pump. These men were sent from the staging area to 48 Poplar, where they found yet another instance of gas odor. They treated this problem as well as another at 13 Poplar and still another at 32 Locust.

Danvers Firefighter Ronnie Moreland was outside his home at 15 Brookside Avenue when he heard a strange noise that sounded like water under pressure running in his basement. Investigating, he got to the top of the cellar stairs where he was met by a blast of gas. He got everyone out including his pets. With a wrench from the garage, he went to the side of his house and shut off the meter. He then went inside and thoroughly aired the house. When he saw Engine 3 arrive at 11 Beaver Park Road, he reported to them and assisted in laying lines.

Our second-shift firefighters when they reported for duty at 3:30 p.m., were assigned to several other engine companies that had been assembled at headquarters. Captain David Sullivan and Captain James Tutko directed operations there. Firefighter Jay Wessell went with the Andover engine company. Firefighter David Cole, with the Boxford engine and crew. Both groups answered calls for gas odor. Cole's group responded to an appeal from 12 Richards Street, after which they checked all houses on Richards, Lindall, and Weston Streets. Two more dwellings were found to have excessive gas leakage.

Lieutenant James McInnis and Firefighter David DeLuca were both assigned to a Beverly pump and sent immediately to the intersection of Oak and School Streets for the same problem. A little later, DeLuca in a Wenham police cruiser reported to Deputy Wessell with fifteen fully charged air bottles. At the Deputy's direction these were unloaded at the Park Lane. There DeLuca donned a mask, entered the building, and started working with Chief Hyde of Swampscott and a Manchester captain in performing general overhaul operations. Firefighter John Duffill, reporting for duty, was sent with Lynn Engine 8. They extinguished a small fire a 10 Page Street and shut off gas at 48 North Putnam, 20 Poplar, and 14R School Streets.

On their return to duty, Firefighters Gerald Mills, Kevin Farley, and Michael Perry manned reserve Engine 4 and reported to the Fair Lane also, where Chief Pelonzi had them set to work in section E, Units 1 and 2. This chief was also directing the work of Beverly Engine 6, Saugus Engine 1, Ipswich Engine 3, and North Reading Ladder 1 at the complex.

A number of units of the Park Lane Condominiums on 15 Lafayette Avenue caught fire and had to be tenaciously put out.

When he heard the news of the fire on his scanner, Lieutenant Robert T. Flachbart was delivering oil in Marblehead. He returned his truck to Salem and proceeded to Engine 3, where he picked up his gear and reported to Captain Sullivan at headquarters. He was assigned to Lynn Engine 9 and later to an Ipswich Company. He checked leaks with them at 36 Spring, 4 East, and 35 and 37 Poplar Streets. By this time the Boston Gas Company had dozens of trucks and crews in the area. They accompanied us to these addresses.

Lieutenant Ted Foster picked up his gear at Engine 2 and got assigned to 192 Maple Street, where he assisted Middleton in getting their lines laid and the roof opened up. Later Deputy Wessell told him to report to the Malden cascade unit. They were, I noted previously, to station themselves between the two condominiums. Later Foster went back to headquarters with Engine 2, where they were sent with the gas company to 21 Locust Street on the report of a strong gas odor. Then they answered what turned out to be a false alarm at the Highland Store at the Danvers Plaza.

As also previously noted, all of our communications—telephone, radio, and fire alarm control—come into and go out of the dispatch center at 120 Ash Street. On duty that afternoon were dispatchers Mo Sullivan and Olivia Silva. Upon the striking of the second alarm, Firefighter/Fire Alarm Technician

William Graves reported here as per procedure to assist them and lend technical advice. Dispatch Supervisor Richard Beaulieu also reported to duty at the center.

This communications center has three stations, but under normal conditions only two are in use—one for fire and the other for police dispatchers. However, in a time of multiple alarms like this day's, the third station is employed. The situation got so hectic on the "fire side" that afternoon that the police house officer had all his phone calls routed to the front desk and by the use of the telephone there and a portable radio, he received and sent out all police communications. Under this arrangement, the dispatch center was left entirely for fire work.

The two on-duty dispatchers, Sullivan and Silva, along with Richard Beaulieu and Bill Graves did an outstanding job. At times the radio traffic was feverish because some of the commanders on the fireground repeatedly requested additional manpower and equipment, and some of that apparatus came from twenty-five miles away. It is quite understandable that a few of our people did get excited and frustrated with the conditions we were working under. (Recall my own impatience with Middleton, whose crew did such a fine job at 192 Maple Street.) But at no time did anyone from the transmission center come over the air in a frantic manner. They handled everything like the professionals they were.

It should be mentioned that one of our strongest support groups had been the Lyons Ambulance Service. Their first response came just three minutes after we received the initial alarm at 3:12 p.m. The Lyons family has been performing this kind of work for over eighty-five years. It all started after William Lyons in 1903 had been injured when his wagon was struck by a Lawrence-bound trolley car. The livery stable he started after that included an ambulance service. His family still runs the business, the only one on the Square run now by the fourth generation.

The following is a chronological report of the Emergency Medical Service actions taken by them and also by the North Shore Ambulance Inc. of Salem:

- 3:15 p.m. Lyons 422 dispatched to area of Lafayette Ave. and Beaver Park on report of explosion and fire.
- 3:18 p.m. Lyons 421 disp. to Lafayette and Beaver Park to transport elderly female to Hunt Hosp.
- 3:25 p.m. Lyons 420 disp. to area of 200 Maple Street for standby.
- 3:26 p.m. Lyons 424 disp. to area of Beaver Pk. and Brookside Ave. for standby at south side of fire scene.
- 3:27 p.m. Lyons Ambulance Service general callback.
- 3:30 p.m. Lyons 424 transports female from 15 Lafayette Ave. to Hunt Hosp.
- 3:34 p.m. North Shore Ambulance 55 disp. to area of Beaver Park and Brookside (covers Venice Street fire).
- 3:45 p.m. Lyons 425 disp. to Hunt Hosp. to investigate possible evacuation.
- 3:57 p.m. North Shore Ambulance 52 disp. to area of Beaver Park and Brookside for standby.
- 3:58 p.m. Lyons 424 clears Hunt Hospital and takes position at Pickering St. and Beaver Park.

4:16 p.m. North Shore Ambulance 55 transports Swampscott firefighter with minor injuries to Salem Hospital.
4:34 p.m. Lyons 421 disp. to 11 Poplar St. on report of pregnant woman overcome by fumes. No Duty. F.D. notified of gas condition in home.
4:53 p.m. Lyons 420 handles smoke inhalation/ exhaustion of Danvers firefighter near its post and transports to Hunt Hospital.
5:15 p.m. North Shore Ambulance 55 and 52 released.
5:47 p.m. Lyons 421 recalled to base.
6:38 p.m. Lyons 420, 421, 424, and 425 released by Danvers Fire Dept.

Ultimately these fires went into ten alarms, our maximum. The total apparatus responding to the fires or staging areas were thirty-two engine companies, eight ladder companies, two squad units, and three cascade units. This amounts to a total of fifty-five fire companies, three ambulances, and fourteen police vehicles from various communities. The total manpower at the height of the fires was one hundred officers and men, and there were additionally forty-seven officers and men at the staging areas. Nine chiefs of departments worked that day. A total of twenty-seven communities responded to our calls for mutual aid:

Amesbury	Haverhill	North Andover
Andover	Ipswich	North Reading
Beverly	Lynn	Peabody
Boxford	Lynnfield	Rockport
Danvers	Malden	Salem
Essex	Manchester-by-the-Sea	Saugus
Georgetown	Marblehead	Swampscott
Gloucester	Middleton	Topsfield
Hamilton	Newburyport	Wenham

Compared to the confusion and wide-spread area covered by this disaster, the next one proved quite a bit tamer for us, although almost as uncomfortable. It happened on a very blustery, cold night, and during the fight, ice quickly formed on everything.

On Thursday December 13, 1990, at 2:45 a.m., fire alarm received a request from Metro Fire, the Boston area dispatch center, for a pump to go to Revere Fire Headquarters. Engine 3 was sent with Lieutenant Robert Flachbart and Firefighters Gerry Mills and Kevin Farrell. As I was apprehensive that this fire might result in another catastrophe, I went also with Lieutenant Michael Skinner.

My suspicions were quite correct. The men from Danvers were dispatched to Highland Street where they worked a 2 1/2"line. This fire consisted of twelve three-story tenement houses and involved three streets. The water volume and pressure were desperately low. Here was a good example of trying to supply too many lines with too little water. Engine 3 returned to quarters later in the morning.

Chief Martin and Lieutenant Skinner experience an oil-drilling rig fire off Gloucester, Massachusetts in December 1990.

CHAPTER XI

Oil Rig and Boat Fires

Newspaper photographs so often show us fighting to save houses, factories, or other buildings that the public has to be reminded that there are occasions when we become seaborne (or riverborne in Danvers) to combat marine disasters.

On Saturday morning, December 16, 1990, at about 5:00 a.m., I received a call from Captain David Sullivan that the U.S. Coast Guard wanted to draw on our foam bank. I had him call the Gloucester Fire Department to confirm the request. That city's dispatcher said that indeed it did need foam and to send all that we could spare to the Gloucester Coast Guard station. We immediately sent Squad 1 with two men and fifty-five gallon containers of 3 percent protein foam.

I responded in the chief's car accompanied by Lieutenant Skinner as I wanted to monitor the use of the foam and also to determine who would resupply our Essex County Foam Bank. At the Gloucester rotary on Route 128, both Squad 1 and we were met by Gloucester police cruiser and escorted to our destination.

On the opposite side of the Gloucester breakwater we could see an oil-drilling rig engulfed in flame and smoke. It had been used to construct the new Gloucester sewerage outflow pipeline. A command post was set up in the conference room of the station where all the people representing the Coast Guard and the fire services were assembled: Rear Admiral Richard Ryback, the first Coast Guard District commander; the captain of the Port of Boston, Captain William Bowland, Jr., who represented the Coast Guard also; Chief Barry McKay, Chief of the Gloucester Fire Department; Chief James Lonergan of the Logan Airport Fire Department, who was in command of the Massport fireboat, *Howard W. Fitzpatrick* ; and I as the one responsible for the foam. The owners of the rig were there also.

It was apparent from the beginning that logistics would be most important as the rig was located two miles out to sea where waves were running three to three and a half feet. The fire had been burning for some four hours. The two men who had been aboard the rig, named *Zeus*, had been rescued by the Coast Guard. It was determined that there were approximately 13,000 gallons of various types of flammable liquid on the rig and that the rig, owned by the Maitlant Brothers of Pennsylvania, was worth about $20M.

The owners of the rig furnished us with detailed blueprints so that we could readily assess the situation. Quite a few suggestions were put forth. I offered my two cents worth by stating that I would let the fire burn itself out, and in that way no one would be subject to injury or death. I can remember so many times we needlessly risked our lives just to save a building that the insurance company would eventually pay for. Another case in point, early on in my career we would have one or two barn fires every year. Many times after spending a day or more attempting to put the barn and the hay out, the farmer would ask permission to finish burning the barn and its contents as the cows would not eat smoked hay. It was cheaper to finish burning the whole mess than to try to repair the barn.

Finally it was agreed that since the rig was less than three miles out to sea and within the city limits, Chief McKay was in charge of firefighting. The Coast Guard supplied transportation and picket duty to keep other vessels at a safe distance. Meanwhile, the first load of foam that we brought from Danvers was put aboard a forty-one foot cutter. We departed from the pier at the Coast Guard station at approximately 8:00 a.m. and headed out to *Zeus*. There was virtually an armada of Coast Guard vessels around us from as far away as Newburyport in the north to Buzzards Bay in the south.

We circled the rig several times observing the damage that had already been done by the fire and conferring again concerning the strategy to be used. Fourteen persons went aboard the *Howard W. Fitzpatrick*, which went in underneath the rig stern first, and the men climbed aboard *Zeus* from there. Lieutenant Skinner was one of the firefighters who did this. He took some very interesting video tapes of the actions aboard the rig for the short period of time they were there. They opened a few vents and hatches to see what was happening down below. Then a severe explosion occurred in the bowels of the rig. All members of the exploration party made a very hasty retreat. After all the brass were back aboard the cutter, the decision was made to return to the station and let the fire burn itself out.

During the action around the rig, I had a camera with me, but the seas were so rough that I feared it might fall from my hands. As I removed my helmet to put the strap around my neck, a young Coast Guard officer offered to hold the helmet while I did this. He observed the color of my hair. Rather hesitantly he said to me, "Excuse me, sir, but may I ask how old you are?"

I replied, "Sixty-four years old. Why?"

"At your age," he said, "what in the hell are you doing out here?"

Thinking about it afterwards, I decided that it was a very good question.

All in all though, it had been quite an exhilarating experience, and one that I will not soon forget, for how many times is a firefighter in New England called upon to extinguish a fire in an oil rig at sea? Boat fires present their own problems also.

Sunday, June 23, 1991, was a glorious summer day. The temperature was in the 70s and the humidity was low. I worked in the garden all day. About 6:00 p.m. I came into the house and was helping my wife Connie prepare supper. Then at 6:36 p.m., the scanner announced that there had been an explosion and fire on a boat in Millet Creek off Parker's Island.

I have witnessed several boat fires over the years. The end result is always one of two extremes. Either the fire is out upon arrival of the department, or it is extinguished at the waterline. I told Connie that I was going to the fire and that I'd be back soon. As I approached the intersection of Maple and Summer Streets, I could see a column of black smoke rising into the sky. My thoughts were confirmed. This fire was going to be extinguished at the waterline.

An explosive boat fire near Parker's Island off Liberty Street on June 23, 1991.

Upon his entering Parker's Island, Captain James Tutko ordered the striking of a second alarm. I parked my car there, put on my helmet and coat, and headed toward the top of the gangplank leading down to the slips. I hesitated there a moment sizing up the situation. There were copious amounts of acrid black smoke, and the flames were leaping up to thirty feet into the air. Two boats approximately thirty-six feet long were fully involved. There were two other boats outboard of them that were partly involved. 1 3/4" lines were being advanced onto the pier but were having little effect on the ferociously burning boats.

I immediately called the electric department to have all power to Parker's Island turned off. Fire alarm informed me that a Coast Guard cutter was responding from Loop Point Station in Gloucester. The estimated time of arrival was another eighteen to twenty minutes. I then walked down the gangplank to the pier where Captain Tutko was working desperately with his men to confine the fire to the boats. This was a very harrowing predicament to be in because the center two boats, which were fully involved, were only inches apart. The outboard of each of these boats is a short finger pier that is only three feet wide.

The water situation soon became serious. For the life of me, I could not understand why we were experiencing a depleting water supply. I ordered Lieutenant Skinner to go up on the island and find out where our water supply was located. We were operating at sea level and should have had a pressure of nearly one hundred pounds minus friction loss. At one time I called for our float pumps to be brought to the scene. Shortly after my request, one did arrive whether by my request or that of others, I do not recall as this was at the height of the fire and everything was in a very confused state.

I also did not know if any of the vessels were gasoline or diesel powered. Preventing explosions was of top priority. I was concerned because one exploding gasoline-fueled tank could destroy a quarter of the Danvers Fire Department.

It seemed like an eternity until Lieutenant Skinner found the valve in the water main on Parker's Island. When it was fully opened, our hose lines began to have an effect on the spreading flames leaping from boat to boat. Shortly thereafter a majestic forty-one foot Coast Guard cutter came up the channel of the Danvers River leaving a tremendous wake as it was not abiding by the no-wake regulation since the Salem/Beverly and the Kernwood Bridge tenders were holding their spans open a period of twenty minutes awaiting the arrival of this vessel. Just imagine what that did to the Sunday evening traffic!

The boat adjacent to the original boat that had caused this fire was slowly sinking below the waters of Millet Creek. With the cutter present, the boat in which the fire originated was cast off under controlled conditions, put out into the channel, and turned around so that the bow was now heading in toward the main pier alongside the finger pier. There was a furious fire still burning in the forward cabin. Captain Robert Cyr and Firefighter Doug Carter standing next to me at the end of the finger pier suggested using a Bresnan nozzle with its nine orifices directing its water stream in various directions. I agreed with them.

We shut down the line we were using, and Firefighter William Trefrey attached the Bresnan nozzle, generally used for cellar fires, to the hose. He then threw the line onto the deck and partially through the hatch to the cabin below. At this time, Doug Conrad and he helped me onto the deck of the boat where I inserted the nozzle farther through the hatch into the cabin. A little later, the cutter attached a line to the stern of this boat, we withdrew our lines, and the Coast Guardsmen towed the still burning vessel out into the Danvers River.

Soon thereafter, the deputy and I boarded our Harbor Master's boat and went over to where the cutter had previously brought the original boat at the foot of Sandy Beach. Realizing that this was the second day of summer and that Sandy Beach would be host to hundreds of youngsters throughout the summer, Deputy Wessell suggested that we beach the boat at the end of Mead Street, where the property is owned by the town, had a hydrant close by, and would involve no legal entanglements. It was not easy feat for the Coast Guard to perform this task, but they did. Engine 3 of Middleton, under the command of Chief George Nash, was there waiting to complete the extinguishment.

Dick Wessell and I returned to the original fire scene and conferred with Captain Jim Tutko, who had informed the Department of Environmental Protection of the situation and also the state fire marshal's office.

As of 1991 the Danvers Fire Department consisted of one chief, one deputy chief, four captains, nine lieutenants, and thirty-six firefighters. One of our lieutenants functioned as a full-time Fire Prevention Officer. We have three engine companies, one ladder company, and one squad in active service. We also have two pumps and one ladder in reserve. All of the above apparatus is in good condition with the exception of reserve Engine 5.

Reflecting over the past forty-five years, I have seen many changes in the fire service. Mostly they have been to the good. Our apparatus is pretty much the same in that a pump carries five hundred gallons of water and has hose carrying capabilities. The greatest change has been in the miscellaneous equipment that we use. Forty-five years ago, our basic equipment was a six-pound axe and a rake. Today we have all types of forcible-entry tools. Years ago, for example, we would take an axe and literally chop our way through a door. Today, we use a jamb-spreader whereby we put this device at the door handle height and using a ratchet lever literally force the two jambs apart thereby releasing the door latch from its pocket. We can then open the door with one finger. We have saws with carbide-tipped teeth which we use to ventilate roofs. This can be accomplished in seconds versus an axe that takes a much longer period of time. These power saws can cut through metal and masonry as well. Our self-contained breathing apparatus permits us to have up to forty-five minutes of air when we are working in smoke-filled or other contaminated atmospheres.

Another of our major advances has been the use of four-inch hoses. We also have an excellent water supply and ample hydrants within the town. By the use of these larger hoses, we virtually lay an above-ground water main from the nearest hydrant to the pump in front of the fire structure. In most cases, we are thus only committing one pump to be out of service at a fire.

Then too there is the fog nozzle. It was developed by the U.S. Navy during World War II and over the years has been improved upon considerably. By the use of this type of nozzle, the water is delivered upon the fire in minute droplet form. The droplets are smaller than the head of a match, and they are readily converted to steam by the heat thus reducing the temperature of the fire and smothering the flames.

Radios play a critical role in our work. In years gone by at a serious fire, the only way to communicate in most instances was by yelling to one another. Our modern portable radios are lightweight and compact. Using them, we can communicate from one floor to another in a building or from Folly Hill to West Street behind the State Hospital.

The new chief who follows me will find his job very challenging but also very rewarding. He will have periods when he will say to himself, "What in hell did I take this job for anyway?" Then there will be other times when he will arrive at a very serious and threatening fire, call for a multiple alarm, and bring the fire fight to a successful conclusion with no injuries. He will look back over the actions of his men at such a particular incident and feel very warm and proud that he had been part of this operation. I personally look at these incidences as adventures, such as the three conflagrations I participated in and the gas fires of April 2, 1990.

Changes in building construction will play a major role in the future. Suppression equipment such as sprinklers will be included in every structure

Leland Martin, John Joseph Farley and James P. Tutko, the three Danvers Chiefs of the last half of the twentieth century, pose for a picture. Their leadership and vision made the Danvers Fire Department the proud, modern department it is today.

including single-family residences. There will be officers of the fire department who will have bachelor's and master's degrees in fire science. They will be the leaders of the fire service of the future.

On a final personal note, let me say that I have always strived to do my best in all my endeavors. In some cases, I have been very successful and in others I have failed, but I have always tried.

Card indicating the fire alarm whistle system as of 1891.

147

The new High Street headquarters was opened and dedicated on October 1, 1995. Department equipment in this March 1997 photo includes from left, Squad 1 (1989), Engine 1 (1996), Engine 4 (1983), Engine 3 (1986) and Ladder 1 (1969).

AFTERWORD

With the retiring of Chief Leland Martin, James P. Tutko was appointed the new fire chief in 1991. Tutko, a Danvers native, had joined the department right out of college in 1971. He later studied fire science at North Shore Community College. In 1982 he became a lieutenant; and in 1989, a captain.

Back in the 1960s and 70s training as a firefighter was mainly on-the-job via the buddy system, whereas today recruits must attend and graduate from the Massachusetts Firefighting Academy. Firefighting is now much more complicated than years ago, due to the composition of plastic and other hazardous materials and chemicals found in modern houses, vehicles, and commercial structures. Safety of the public and firefighters is paramount in the profession, and the best way to assure safety is through fire prevention. Remarks Chief Tutko, "My philosophy is if I can prevent a fire before it starts, I don't have to put people in danger after it's going. That includes the general public as well as the firefighters themselves." Regular inspections of buildings, in-house training sessions for firefighters and public and school education in fire safety are all means employed by the Danvers department to this end.

A major event in the history of the Danvers Fire Department occurred on Sunday, October 1, 1995. After many years of discussions, planning, design and construction, the new fire headquarters on High Street was dedicated. The *Danvers Herald* noted that what made the opening ceremonies memorable was, "combining an appreciation of the past with an optimistic nod to the future."

The need for a new fire headquarters had been bandied about for almost twenty-five years. During the 1980s, Chief Martin had suggested to Town Manager Wayne Marquis that a site on High Street between the Central Fire House and the Engine 3 station in Danversport would be appropriate, and allow for the consolidation of apparatus and the closing of these two old stations. The site chosen was at 62–66 High Street, where a BMW auto dealership had expanded the building after acquiring the property in 1988. The land and building were purchased for $1 million following approval by Danvers Town Meeting in June 1994. The structure was then dismantled down to its steel skeleton, roof and cement floor. The architect firm for the new station was Donham & Sweeney of Cambridge with R. C. Griffin of Peabody as contractor and David Anderson and Robert Gnoza, the latter a former Danvers firefighter, as job representatives. Retired Danvers Public Works Director Newton Sweet served as clerk of the works and an internal committee of town firefighters and a representative community Building Design and Construction Advisory Committee worked diligently to make the brick and steel building user friendly including up-to-date safety features and utility areas.

The $1.9 million project included a large and spacious apparatus area with a plymovent system whereby the diesel vehicle exhaust is vented and not allowed to permeate the station. On the main floor are administrative offices; a repair area; a decontamination area with shower, eyewash and sinks; and a room to keep gear on open racks in a vented and climate controlled area. On the second floor, which runs around the apparatus bay, there are evidence and conference rooms, including a multi-purpose training room, a record storage area, sleeping areas and a full service kitchen. The building is also equipped with a heavy-duty generator. In front of the structure is a ninety foot driveway allowing the apparatus to turn around and back in without tying up traffic on High Street.

At the fall dedication event town officials, guests, and present and past firefighters mustered at the old Locust Street Central Fire Station accompanied by a bagpipe band and the 1936 Danvers Pirsch Engine 4 now owned and beautifully restored by Southborough resident Peter Faneuf. A final whistle rang out "341" to close the station. After a march to the new station, "1464," the new designation for headquarters, was rung in. Firefighter Mike Perry, President of the Danvers Firefighters' Relief Association, rededicated the granite memorial to deceased firefighters located near the new headquarters entrance. This memorial had originally been installed and dedicated in 1991 at the Locust Street Station and was carefully moved to its new location. The monument, made out of African Black granite in the shape of a monolith, is carved with an image of a firefighter's badge and of a steam engine on flight to a fire. The memorial is inscribed, "Danvers Fire Department. Erected in grateful memory to our members who have served with courage and devotion. Dedicated June 9, 1991, by the Relief Association of the Danvers Fire Department, founded October 1894. June 11, 1995." The roll of the names of deceased firefighters was announced by representative members of the department, followed by the word "recall" and by the twice clanging of a bell.

In the fall of 1996 the department received its first new apparatus since 1989, a Quint fire truck. Costing $343,000, the truck is the first of its kind used in Danvers. Included in its red and white painted Emergency One body is a pump truck, hose wagon, water tank, ground ladder carrier and seventy-five foot aerial ladder. Needing only one driver and no tillerman, as in the case with traditional ladder trucks, the Quint ladder can also be extended straight out parallel to the ground for ice rescues and the like without danger of the ladder snapping. Also serving as a pumper, the vehicle can carry seven firefighters and all their gear.

In July 1997, Deputy Chief Richard Wessell retired after thirty-three years of service. Captain Stephen Prendergast, who joined the department in 1973, was appointed the new Deputy Fire Chief in September 1997.

Approaching the close of the twentieth century, the Danvers Fire Department remains in the forefront of technology, taking advantage of new techniques in fire education and firefighting. Stressing prevention and knowing the increased dangers of fire and the potential deadly results of toxic fumes released by almost any fire, firefighters still must rely on their individual courage, physical prowess, knowledge, training and comradeship to take on their powerful rival. We can all be thankful that no matter the danger and fury, or the medical emergency, we have such a well trained Fire Department to serve us and our community.

R. B. T.

In 1996 Danvers purchased its first "Quint" truck, which is a combination pump truck, hose wagon, water tank, ground ladder carrier and seventy-five foot ladder truck. Designated Engine 1, the vehicle rolls out of headquarters on High Street.

152

Members of Major Chase Hose Company 4 pose with their equipment around their two-wheel hose reel in this ca. 1880s photograph.

APPENDIX ONE
Compiled by Richard B. Trask with the assistance of Richard C. Wessell

A list of major firefighting Danvers Fire Department

Year Acquired	Original Number or Name	Manufacturer	Price
1800	Federal 1	Ephraim & Stephen Thayer Boston, MA	
1800	Danvers 2	Ephraim & Stephen Thayer	
1822	Niagara 1	Hunneman & Co. Boston, MA	$500
1822	Danvers 2	Hunneman & Co.	$500
1830	Torrent 3	Hunneman & Co.	$575
1837	General Putnam 4	Samuel Huse & Co. Newburyport, MA	$750
1837	Eagle 5	Samuel Huse & Co.	$575
1844	Ocean 6	E. S. Lesley Newburyport, MA	$775
1844	General Foster 7	E. S. Lesley	$775
1845	Volunteer 8	Lysander Button & Co. Waterford, NY	10 year loan
1849	Torrent 3	Hunneman & Co.	$694
1850	General Scott 2	E. S. Lesley	$850

apparatus acquired by the from 1800 through 1997

Original Location	Remarks
South Parish Near Bell Tavern	A receiving engine
New Mills (Danversport)	A receiving engine.
South Parish Main Street	Replaced Federal. Moved to West Peabody in the 1860s. Sold in 1869.
New Mills (Danversport)	Replaced the 1800 Danvers 2 engine. Renamed the Erie, Reformer and Albion in the 1830s.
South Parish Central Street	Now preserved at the Waldoborough Historical Society, Waldoboro, ME.
Danvers Plains	Named after General Israel Putnam.
South Parish Main Street	
New Mills (Danversport)	The 1822 Company 2 engine was moved from New Mills to the emerging Tapley Village section of town and renamed General Scott.
South Parish Lowell Street	Engine named after militia general and Revolutionary War veteran Gideon Foster.
South Parish Main Street	Side stroke engine given on loan by Gen. William Sutton.
South Parish	6 1/8" cylinder. Replaced 1830 Company 3 engine.
Tapleyville	6 1/2" cylinder, end stroke engine. Sold old Company 2 engine for $210.

1854	Volunteer 8	Lysander Button & Co.	$1,100
1855	Town of Danvers split into Town of Danvers and Town of South Danvers. Danvers retained Engines 2, 4, and 6.		
1858	Town of Danvers changed engine numbers. General Putnam Company 4 became Company 1, General Scott remained Company 2, and Ocean Company 6 became Company 3.		
1872	General Putnam 1	Lysander Button & Co.	$1,985
1874	Danvers 1	Hunneman & Co.	$4,849
1874 (1855)	Ocean 3	Lysander Button & Co.	$500
1876	Town of Danvers opens a pressurized municipal piped water system. Steamer and hand pumps become obsolete.		
1877	3 hose carriages	Edward B. Leverick New York	$250 each
1878	Hose carriage	Hunneman & Co.	$85
1878	2 hose carriages	James T. Ryan & Co.	$133 each
1883	Hook & Ladder	Second-hand purchase from Peabody, MA.	$350
1891	3 hose wagons	Dole & Osgood Peabody, MA.	$300 each
1892	Hook & Ladder	Rumsey Manufacturing Co.	$1,400
1899	Hose Wagon 4	Pike & Whipple	$330
1911	Combination 1	Knox	$2,000
1916	Engine 1	Ahrens-Fox	$8,500
1925	Hose Companies 5, 6, 7, 8, and 9 disbanded at midnight, April 30, 1925.		
1925	Engine 3	Ahrens-Fox	$12,500

South Parish Main Street	Replaced the engine loaned by Gen. Sutton. Included brass mounted hose cart ($85 additional) and 396' single riveted hose ($336 additional). Now preserved by the East Greenwich, R.I. Veteran Firemens' Association.
Danvers Plains	10' cylinder, double air chamber. Replaced 1837 engine. Sold to Weymouth, MA in 1878 for $900. Presently in New England Fire and History Museum, Brewster, MA.
Danvers Plains Maple Street	Second class steam fire engine, Danvers' first and only. Sold in 1877 to Holbrook, MA, for $2,025.
Danversport	This was an 1855 10' cylinder, single air chamber engine built for Westfield, MA and named "Rough and Ready." It was sold by Danvers in 1878 for $400, and was destroyed in a 1963 fire.

Eight hose companies established, becoming nine in 1878.

Danvers Centre	For company 5.
School Street & Sylvan Street	For companies 4 and 9.
Maple Street	There was an earlier Hook & Ladder truck from the 1870s. This carriage was sold in 1892 for $25. To replace 3 four-wheeled reel carriages in companies 1, 2, and 3.
Maple Street	Truck with horse hitch. Included 8 ladders from 10' to 46' long, and 2 roof ladders.
School Street	
School Street	Motorized combination chemical and hose wagon. Included two 35 gal. chemical tanks. Vehicle was hand cranked and chain driven. Replaced Hose Wagon 4. Was retired from service in 1936.
School Street	Motorized pump and hose wagon. Double piston, 800 gpm. pump. Replaced Hose Wagon 1. Was retired from service in 1948.
High Street	Located at new High Street station. Ocean 3 Hose Wagon withdrawn from service. Engine 3 was a triple combination pump, chemical and hose auto Pumped 750 gpm. Was retired from service in 1953.

Year	Unit	Make	Cost
1925	Engine 2	Ahrens-Fox	$8,800
1925	Ladder Truck 1	Ahrens-Fox City Service	$9,500
1930	Foam Truck	Pierce Arrow	
1936	Engine 4	Peter Pirsch	$5,477
1940 (1937)	Engine 6	Dodge	
1940 (1936)	Engine 7	Chevrolet	
1944	Ladder Truck	Ahrens-Fox City Service	borrowed
1947	Ladder Truck 1	Peter Pirsch	$16,500
1948	Engine 1	American LaFrance	$15,500
1951	Engine 2	American LaFrance	$17,100
1954	Engine 3	American LaFrance	
1962	Engine 4	American LaFrance	$23,505
1965	Squad 1		$2,015
1969	Ladder Truck 1	Peter Pirsch	$56,931
1971	Engine 1	Ward LaFrance	$43,076
1971	Squad 1	General Motors	
1973	Engine 1	Ward LaFrance	$51,700
1979	Squad 1	General Motors	$8,266
1979	Engine 1	Continental Firetrucks Hopkinton, MA	$56,462
1983	Engine 3	Emergency One Fire Apparatus of Florida	$89,891
1986	Engine 1	Emergency One	$128,120
1986	Reserve Ladder 2	Peter Pirsch	$20,000
1989	Engine 1	Emergency One	$165,000
1989	Squad 1	Ford F350	$15,975
1996	Engine 1	Emergency One	$343,000

Holten Street	Gen. Scott Hose Wagon 2 withdrawn from service. Engine 2 was a 500 gpm pump. Was retired from service in 1951.
Locust Street	Located at new Central Fire Station with Engine 1 and Combination 1. In 1944 the cylinder block cracked rendering the truck inoperable.
Locust Street	Truck converted by George Jones, Sr. to carry foam-maker, foam and hose.
Locust Street	600 gpm. triple combination pump. Was retired from service in 1962.
Locust Street	Converted half-ton pickup truck into a grass fire truck carrying 5 gal. hand operated water pumps and a skid pump.
	Converted one-ton pickup truck by P. J. Woods of Topsfield, MA into a grass fire truck with a 500 gal. front mounted pump and 410 gal. booster tank.
Locust Street	Borrowed from Cambridge, MA until a new ladder truck could be purchased.
Locust Street	65' aerial ladder. Placed on reserve in 1969, sold to a collector in 1988.
Locust Street	1,000 gpm. V-12 engine, cab in front of engine and front axle.
Holten Street	1,000 gpm.
High Street	1,000 gpm.
Locust Street	1,000 gpm. Sold to a collector in 1989.
Locust Street	Three-quarter ton pickup. Replaced in 1971.
Locust Street	100' aerial ladder. Tractor replaced in 1983.
Locust Street	1250 gpm. Known as "Moby Dick" because of white color. Renumbered Engine 3 in 1973.
Locust Street	Three-quarter ton pickup.
Locust Street	1250 gpm. Painted yellow.
Locust Street	One-ton pickup.
Locust Street	1,000 gpm. single-stage pump. Commercial chassis. By 1990 designated Engine 4 and a reserve pump.
High Street	Commercial chassis. Reserve pump Engine 4 in 1997.
Locust Street	1250 gpm. All aluminum construction. Engine 3 in 1997.
	Beverly, MA. 100' aerial ladder truck sold to Danvers. Scrapped in 1991.
Locust Street	1250 gpm. Enclosed four-door cab, engine in rear. Engine 2 in 1997.
Locust Street	One-ton four wheel pickup. In service in 1997.
High Street	Located at new headquarters on High Street. Known as a Quint truck, it serves as a pump, hose wagon, water tanker, ground ladder carrier and a 75' ladder truck.

The 1916 Ahrens-Fox engine.

The 1925 Ahrens-Fox Engine 3 at High Street near the end of its career.

A tenacious fire in the 1970s at Waterlac Company on Route 114 is attacked by "Moby Dick." The engine's deck gun, as well as a portable deck gun on the ground, were brought into play.

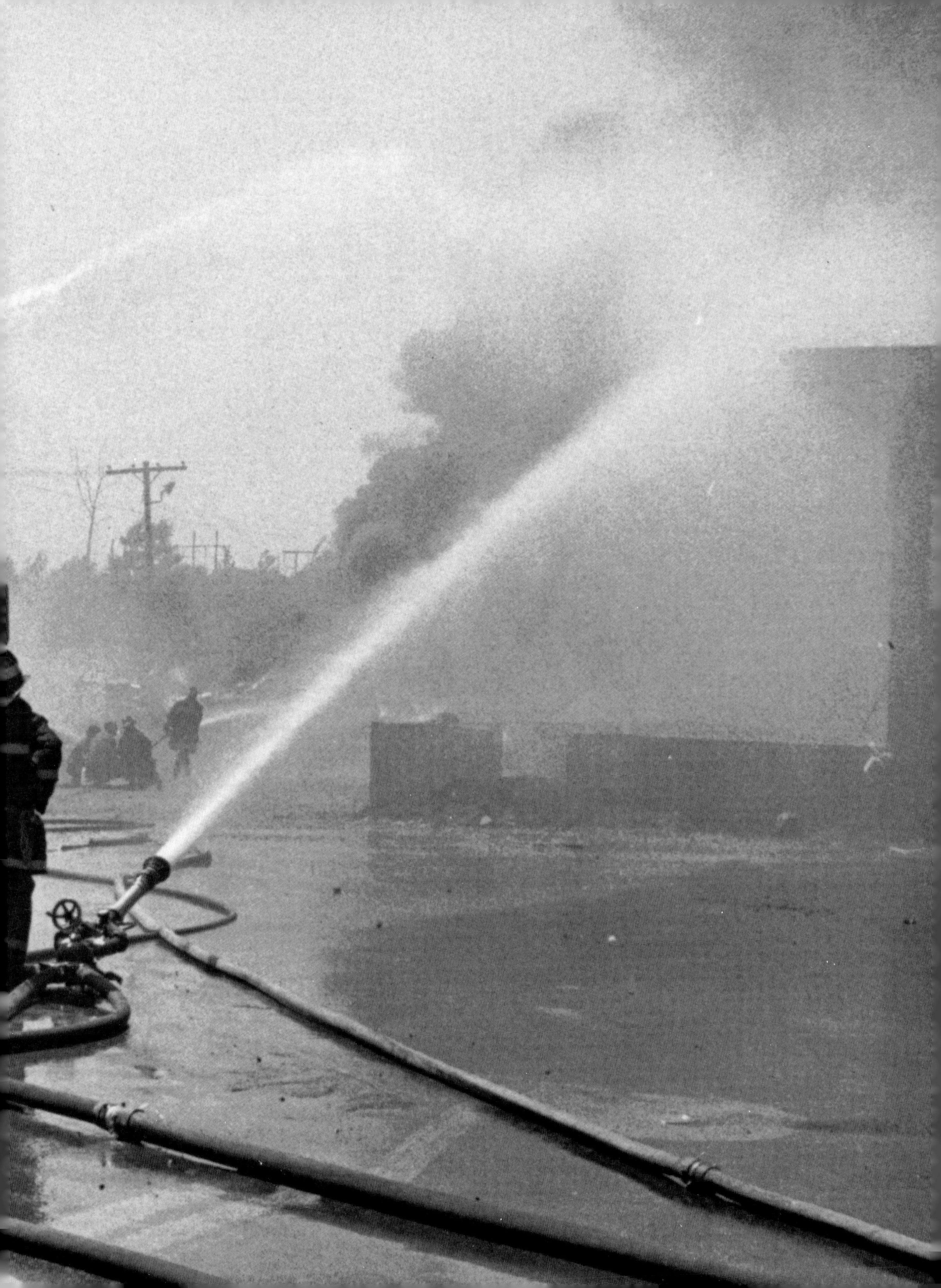

APPENDIX TWO

Firemen 1900–1910

The following is a list of Danvers Firemen who were approved for service by the Board of Engineers during the first decade of the twentieth century. This decade was during the era of the hose wagons, hose reels and hook & ladder wagon. Between six and twelve men were assigned to each company depending upon the type of vehicle. Some of these men served as firefighters for only a year, while a number of others served for many years. In 1910 the town of Danvers voted to purchase its first motorized vehicle, a benchmark event beginning the rapid professionalism and modernization of the department. Some of the men in this list served as firefighters through the 1920s. Their name will not be repeated on other listings.

Aiken, Arthur A.
Barry, James P.
Beals, George E.
Berry, Everett N.
Blaisdell, J. Albert
Blake, Henry J.
Blodgett, Albert W.
Boardman, Leslie P.
Bruley, Joseph W.
Brummitt, Fredrick A.
Brummitt, John D.
Buckman, Allen L.
Butler, Warren H.
Butler, William H.
Caird, Frank H.
Carroll, Phillip
Carver, Angus P.
Casey, Charles M.
Caskin, John A.
Chase, Benjamin F.
Chase, Frank W.
Chase, George S.
Clark, Joshua W.
Clark, N. Perley
Collins, John P.
Connors, Dennis J.

Cowdery, Arthur E.
Crosby, B. Frank
Crosby, George C.
Crosby, S. L.
Cross, Roscoe W.
Curtis, George W.
Curtis, John
Curtis, Oscar L.
Dale, John W.
Dale, William
Danforth, Francis E.
Dennett, Clarence
Dikman, Gilbert
Doane, Melbourne P.
Dougherty, W. W.
Dowdell, James L.
Dowdell, John H.
Dowdell, William
Doyle, Daniel J.
Doyle, Jeremiah M.
Doyle, John E.
Doyle, Maurice J.
Doyle, W. J.
Dunnells, Lorenzo
Dunnells, Walter S.
Eaton, Irvin S.

Faulkner, Daniel D.
Ferguson, Charles F.
Ferguson, F. T.
Ferguson, William H.
Fitzsimmons, Edward F.
Flynn, Michael J.
Foote, John C.
Gates, Samuel L.
George, James F.
Giles, Charles S.
Goldthwait, L. W.
Goodale, J. Walter
Goodale, Loring B.
Gould, Austin L.
Griffin, Eben J.
Griffin, Frank
Ham, Herbert C.
Hanson, John E.
Hatch, O.
Hawks, George A.
Hilton, Harry L.
Hilton, Leaman S.
Hobbs, Edwin B.
Hooper, George D.
Horgan, James A.
Hutchinson, Alfred P.

Hutchinson, F. P.
Jelison, J. Walter
Johnson, Harry G.
Jones, George E., Sr.
Jones, Perley E.
Jones, Theodore E.
Kelly, Edward H.
Kimball, Frank W.
Lachance, Ernest J.
Lindell, A.
Little, George
Littlefield, Austin L.
Lynch, John P.
Lyons, William C.
MacDonald, James
Mains, James H.
Manning, John
Martin, William W.
McCarthy, David F.
McCarthy, John F.
McDonald, W. M.
McKeigue, Frank
McKinnon, Charles H.
Miller, John T.
Moriarty, Daniel D.
Moriarty, John J.
Morrell, William A.
Morrison, Herbert E.
Morse, George M.
Moser, Joseph W.
Murphy, J. J.
Neal, Timothy A.
Neal, William F.
Nightingale, J. Ellis
Nimblett, Frank D.
Nimblett, Leo D.
Nimblett, William F.
O'Brian, John H.
O'Keefe, Jeremiah
Olmstead, L. W.
Peabody, Ralph P.

Pennell, Warren
Perley, Osborn
Perry, Charles H.
Phinney, Byron
Pitman, H. W.
Pitman, Jacob B.
Porter, Walter E.
Powers, John J.
Price, Edward R.
Putnam, Burton L.
Putnam, Edward E.
Rackliff, Walter F.
Reid, Peter
Reid, William
Rigby, George J.
Rundlett, George O.
Russell, Austin S.
Russell, Edmund N.
Russell, Percy E.
Russell, Walter J.
Ryan, Michael J.
Shackley, Clarence
Shea, John F.
Shea, Patrick J.
Sleeper, Albert C.
Smith, Frederick
Spears, Edward J.
Sprout, John
Staples, Charles H.
Staples, George E.
Steele, Leslie J.
Steutermann, John H.
Studley, George
Sullivan, David J.
Sullivan, John F.
Sullivan, P. J.
Sullivan, Timothy J.
Sweetser, Frank E.
Swindell, Elden A.
Thibodeau, Adolphus
Tibbetts, Charles A.

Volunteer fireman Benjamin F. Chase was born in 1861. A well known handler of horses, Chase served as a driver for the fire department for thirty-eight years. He retired from service on October 1, 1925, when the horse drawn hook and ladder truck was retired from service.

Tibbetts, Willard P.
Tibbetts, William F.
Townsend, Harry S.
Trask, Percy C.
Tufts, Aaron P.
Tufts, Lester B.
Tufts, Sherman, A.
Walker, Charles H.
Walker, Watson J.
Walker, William H.
Webb, Ernest S.
White, Harvey E.
Whitman, Carl N.
Williams, Chester
Williams, George E.
Woodman, Frank B.
Wrest, George
Yates, James

APPENDIX THREE

Firefighters of the 20th Century

This list is a compilation of names of firefighters, both permanent and call, who served one or more years in the department through 1996. Not included on the list are duplicate names from the 1900-1910 firefighters list, nor of men who are on the current duty roster of the Fire Department.

Amnott, Clarence H.
Ayers, William C.
Barrows, Albert S.
Barry, Bernard L.
Barry, Michael H.
Battye, George W.
Begin, Jacob J.
Begin, Raymond J.
Belcher, William W.
Berry, William A.
Bialecki, Joseph J.
Blodgett, Fred W.
Blute, Charles A.
Blute, John J.
Bond, Rufus
Bouras, Charles J., Jr.
Bradstreet, Hollis R.
Brown, George M.
Brown, Paul
Bruley, Roger
Bullard, Edwin
Butler, William H.
Casey, Benjamin W.
Caskin, John M.
Cassidy, George V.
Citroni, Dominic R.
Citroni, Roland R.
Clark, Hobart

Clemons, W.
Cole, W.
Coleman, William J., Jr.
Collins, Charles Leonard
Collins, H. E.
Collins, Walter J.
Condon, William J.
Conley, Percy
Cook, Alfred A.
Cook, Clifford B.
Cook, Frank R.
Crossman, Ralph T.
Crowley, John E.
Cyr, Robert J.
Davis, Philip W.
DeCoff, George E.
Doyle, Charles H.
Duke, the Dog
Dwinell, Francis W.
Eaton, Carl E.
Eisenhaur, Harold
Elliot, John A.
Ellsworth, Roland W.
Ennis, James F., Jr.
Falvey, John J.
Farley, John
Farley, John Joseph
Farrell, John J.

Ferguson, Edward A.
Ferguson, Ralph W.
Finnegan, P. Francis
Finnegan, Patrick F.
Flynn, William J.
Ford, Arthur M.
Ford, Michael A.
Foster, Theodore E.
Gaffney, Gerard A.
Gallivan, Patrick A.
Gauthier, Mary J.
Gilbo, Francis
Gilmor, R. J., Jr.
Gilmore, Robert H.
Giroux, Charles T.
Gnoza, Robert P.
Guppy, Raymond
Haggerty, John F.
Harrigan, Arthur I.
Hartman, Edwin T.
Hawkins, Laurice R.
Hayes, Wilbert K.
Heaphy, William
Hicks, David W.
Hilton, Clarence
Homan, Harold G.
Horgan, James M.
Horgan, John J.

166

Huntley, J. F.
Jones, George E., Jr.
Jones, Gordon C.
Jordan, Fred S.
Joyce, Robert J., Jr.
Joyce, Robert J., Sr.
Keefe, Jeremiah J.
Kelley, W. E.
Kelley, Joseph E., Jr.
Kelley, Joseph E., Sr.
Kenell, Charles H.
King, Melvin E.
Kinsella, Joseph M.
Kuell, Alfred H.
Kuell, Charles H., Jr.
La Fortune, Arthur P.
LaChance, Arthur T.
LaChance, George N.
LaChance, Joseph
LaPointe, Ronald
Lawton, Bert
Lear, James J.
Linehan, David J.
Lord, Arthur R.
Lynch, John P.
Lyons, Bernard P.
Lyons, Jerimiah P.
MacLean, Valentine P.
Madison, James V.
Madison, John D.
Manning, Donald P.
Maple, Fred J.
Maple, Thomas E.
Martin, Christopher
Martin, Leland E., Jr.
Martin, Walter
Maynard, Francis O.
Maynard, Leo F.
McFarland, Fred
McInnis, C. E., Jr.
McInnis, Charles

McInnis, James A.
McLaughlin, Edward F.
Modest, Walter B.
Monty, F.
Moreland, Ronald L.
Morin, Sylvio J.
Morrissey, John
Mugridge, Parker P.
Mugridge, Wallace M.
Mullaly, Charles D.
Mullaly, Harold T.
Murphy, William F.
Neary, Matthew F.
Nimblett, B. T.
Nimblett, Charles J.
Nimblett, Leo D.
Noonan, John M.
Osgood, Richard K.
Osgood, Robert G.
Pearson, William B.
Pennell, Everett E.
Pennell, Lloyd E.
Pennell, Wilson H.
Perry, Sarafine F.
Pettipas, John B.
Phinney, James H.
Pierce, Stephen
Pitman, Ralph E.
Pollard, Charles A., Jr.
Price, David E.
Pyburn, Robert J., Sr.
Ransom, Harold A.
Regan, Francis D.
Rigby, William E.
Riggs, John, Jr.
Robinson, Henry P.
Rock, Percy
Rowe, Frederick
Russell, Vernon C.
Ryan, Joseph R.
Ryan, William B.

Santorella, Anthony D.
Santorella, Joseph, Jr.
Sargent, George A.
Scanlon, Kirk R.
Sheppard, Eli
Simpson, Charles E.
Simpson, Charles J.
Skinner, Harold
Skinner, Hollis G.
Skinner, Michael C.
Skinner, Walton F.
Small, Frank J.
Small, James H.
Smith, Earl W.
Smith, P. G.
Smith, Wayne G.
Spears, Thomas F.
Sprague, E. Walter, Jr.
Sturtevant, Roland F.
Sullivan, David C.
Sullivan, James F.
Sullivan, Raymond A.
Swindell, Frederick W.
Talbot, Francis H.
Talbot, Henry J.
Thomas, Henry H.
Trask, Gardner S.
Tufts, Arthur S.
Vaillancourt, Wilfred A.
Wallace, Hardy P.
Weaver, William J.
Whalen, James E.
White, Joseph E.
Williams, Myron A.
Wilkins, Frank A.
Wilson, George A.

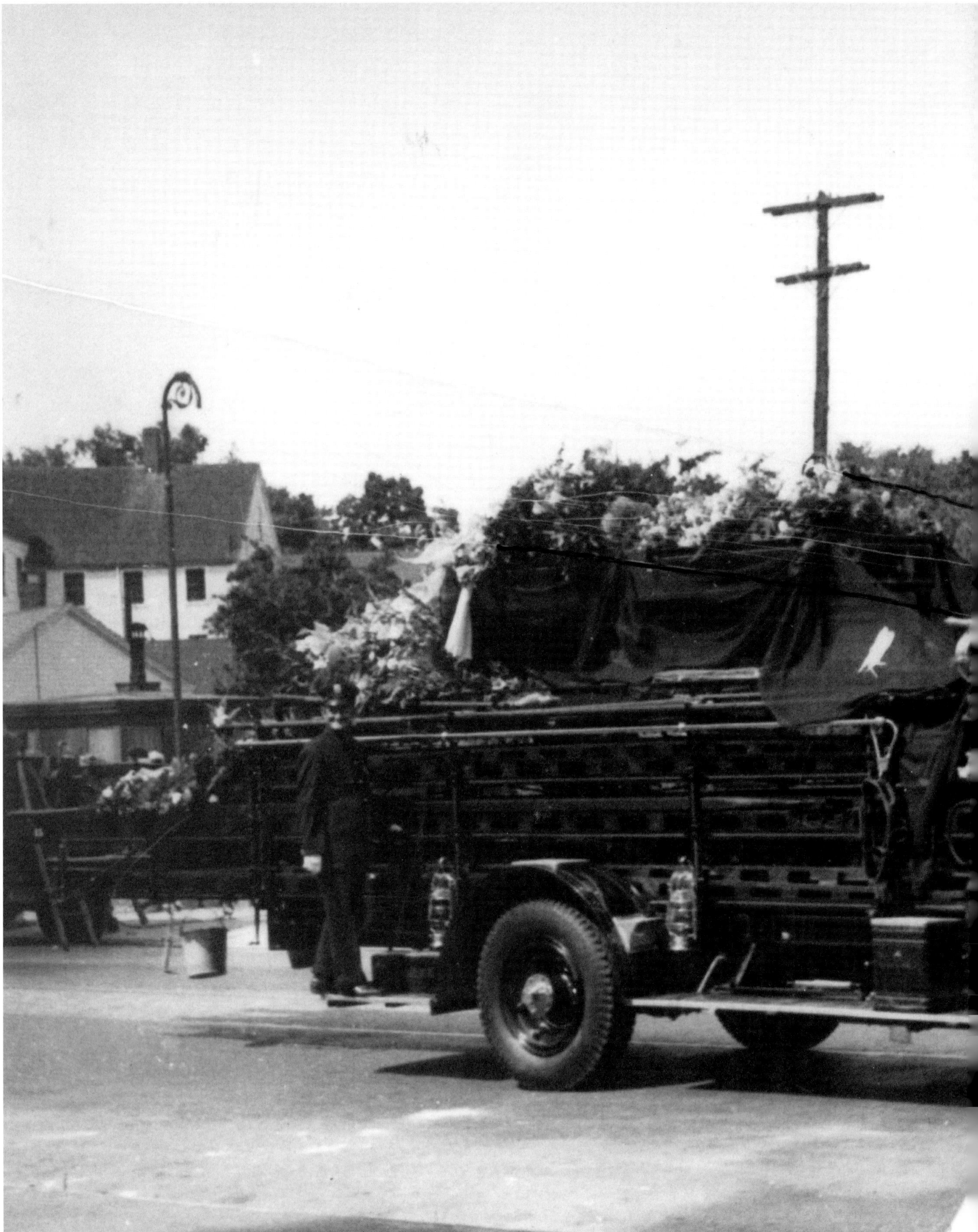

The Ahrens-Fox ladder truck served in the funeral procession for firefighter Hollis Skinner in July 1937. Driver John Madison and William Pearson pass by the front of the Maple Street Church.

APPENDIX FOUR

Duty Roster for the 1997 Danvers Fire Department

Chief James P. Tutko
Deputy Richard C. Wessell

Group 1

Headquarters

Captain	Arnold L. Cyr
Firefighter	John W. Duffill, Jr.
Firefighter	William G. Graves
Firefighter	Barry Hobey
Firefighter	Robert Parsons
Firefighter	Michael E. Perry

Engine 2

Lieutenant	Robert Pyburn
Firefighter	Michael Farley
Firefighter	Robert A. LaPointe

Engine 3

Lieutenant	Douglas Conrad
Firefighter	Jeffrey J. Harrison
Firefighter	Francis Toomey

Group 2

Headquarters

Captain	Robert T. Flachbart
Firefighter	Richard D. Kennedy
Firefighter	Ronald B. Skinner
Firefighter	Matthew Smith
Firefighter	Arnold N. Weeks, Jr.

Engine 2

Lieutenant	James Brooks
Firefighter	Marc Smorczewski
Firefighter	David L. Sullivan

Engine 3

Lieutenant	Frank Sacco
Firefighter	Robert Amerault
Firefighter	David Morin

Group 3

Headquarters

Captain	Richard J. Sullivan
Firefighter	Brian Barry
Firefighter	David Cole
Firefighter	Edward McLaughlin
Firefighter	Ford R. Smith
Firefighter	DeWayne Sullivan

Engine 2

Lieutenant	Richard T. Chase
Firefighter	Michael Graves
Firefighter	George H. Snow

Engine 3

Lieutenant	Kevin Farrell
Firefighter	Kevin J. Farley
Firefighter	Frederick Ingraham

Group 4

Headquarters

Captain	Stephen L. Prendergast
Firefighter	Paul LaPointe
Firefighter	Gerald R. Millis
Firefighter	Albert F. Petronzio
Firefighter	Henry T. Tutko
Firefighter	Jay Wessell

Engine 2

Lieutenant	Alan Weeks
Firefighter	Kenneth Kobierski
Firefighter	Nicholas Serratore

Engine 3

Lieutenant	James McPherson
Firefighter	Richard T. Pyburn
Firefighter	William Trefrey

Fire Prevention

Lieutenant David R. DeLuca

Secretary	Christine M. Perry

INDEX

A
Ahrens-Fox, 48, *49*, 50, *52*, *54*, 55, *59*, 64, *70*, 72, *73*, 156, 158, *160*, *161*, *169*
Aiken, Arthur A., 164
Albion, 20, 155
Allard, Jay, 46
Allison, Steven, 133
Allphin, Willard, 13
Almy's Department Store, 102
Amerault, Robert, 170
American LaFrance, 66, 76, 77, 87, *91*, 118, 158
Amesbury, Mass., 139
Amnott, Clarence H., 50, *52*, *54,* 166
Anderson, David, 149
Andover, Mass., 136, 139
As the Century Turned: Photographic Glimpses of Danvers, 1880–1910, 11
Avery, C. W., 13
Ayers, William C., 86, 166

B
Babco Industries, 107
Bacheller, Everett, 69
Baptist Church, 23, 25, 28, 29
Barrows, Albert S., 166
Barry, Bernard L., 166
Barry, Brian, 171
Barry, James P., 164
Barry, Michael H., 46, 48, 50, 166
Barry, Richard, 97
Batcheldor, Captain, 35
Batchelder's Ice House, 6, 57
Battye, George W., 46, 166
Beals, George E., 164
Bean, Theodore, 64
Beaulieu, Richard, 138
Beaver Park, 11, 123, 125, 138
Begin, Jacob J., 166
Begin, Raymond J., 166
Belcher, William W., 166
Bell Tavern, 17, 155
Bell's Hall, 39
Bell, George W., 39
Benner, David, 13
Berry Tavern, 32
Berry, Everett N., 164
Berry, Max, 8, 95, 97
Berry, William A., 46, 56, 95 32, *44*, *47*, 91, 166
Beverly Airport, *107*
Beverly, Mass., 34, 56, 63, 85, 93, 95, 102, 110, 110, 113, 117, 119, 127, 129, 130, 131, 136, 136, 139, 144, 159
Bialecki, Joseph J., 166
Billy-B-Damns, 8
Blaisdell, J. Albert, 164
Blake, Henry J., 164

Blodgett, Albert W., *44*, 164
Blodgett, Fred W., 56, 166
Blosofsky, Laura, 7
Blosofsky, Mr., 7
Blute, Charles A., 166
Blute, John J., 166
Board of Engineers, 164
Board of Firewards, 19
Boardman, Leslie P., 164
Bond, Rufus, 166
Borsetti, Michael, 110
Boston Fire Department Band, 76
Boston Fire Department, 50
Boston Gas Company, 124, 126, 133, 137
Boston Harbor, 79
Boston, Mass., 139
Bouras, Charles J., Jr., 166
Bowland, William, Jr., 141
Boxford, Mass., 7, 63, 136, 139
Boy Scouts, 59
Bradbury, Steve, 13
Bradstreet, Hollis R., 166
Brennan, Jim, 8
Briggs, Joseph F., 13
Brooks, James, 133, 135, 170
Brown, Amos, 33
Brown, George M., 166
Brown, Paul, 166
Brown, Thurl D., *40*
Bruley, Joseph W., 164
Bruley, Roger, 166
Brummitt, Fredrick A., 164
Brummitt, John D., 164
Bryson, Peter, 88
Bucket brigades, 17
Buckman, Allen L., 164
Buff, Sheila, 12
Bullard, Edwin, 166
Butler, Warren H., 164
Butler, William H., 164, 166
Button & Co., Lysander, 24, *37*, 38, 39, 41, 154, 156

C
Cahill, Bill, 12, 96
Cahill, Jim, 79
Caird, Frank H., 164
Caliga, Joseph, 64
Cambridge, Mass., 159
Carbone, Francis J., 13
Carroll, Phillip, 164
Carter, Doug, 144
Carver, Angus P., 164
Casey, Benjamin W., 166
Casey, Charles M., 164
Caskin, John A., 164
Caskin, John M., 166
Cassidy, George V., 166

Cedar Junction, Mass., 118
Central Falls, Rhode Island, *26*
Central Fire Station, 16, 48, 50, *51*, *52*, 53, *54*, 55, *59*, 77, 78, 85, 92, 130, 149, 159
Chase, Benjamin F., *44*, 46, 164
Chase, Frank W., 164
Chase, George S., 164
Chase, Richard T., 115, 129, 131, 132, 133, *135, 171*
Chelsea, Mass., 105, 106, 110, 111
Chevrolet, 58, *59*, 104, 158
Chicago, 6
Chief Engineer, 19
Cistern, 23, *24*, *34*
Citizens' Hose Company, *74*, 75, 78
Citroni, Dominic R., 166
Citroni, Roland R., 166
Civil Defense Corps, 59
Civil War, 36
Clark, Hobart, 166
Clark, Joshua W., 164
Clark, N. Perley, 164
Clement, Clarence, 56
Clemons, W., 166
Clougherty, John, 7, 110, 129
Coast Guard, 141, 142, 143, 144
Cole, David, 136, 171
Cole, W., 166
Coleman, William J., Jr., 56, 166
Collins, Charles Leonard, *85*, *91*, 91, 93, 166
Collins, H. E., 166
Collins, John P., 164
Collins, Michael F., Father, 63
Collins, Toni, 11, 13
Collins, Walter J., 166
Columbian Fire Club, 17
Combination, 47, 48, *49*, 50, 55, 57, 87, 156, 157
Condon, William J., 166
Conley, Percy, 166
Connelly's Candy Store, 111
Connors, Dennis J., 164
Conrad, Douglas, 144, 170
Continental Fire Trucks, 109, 158
Conway, William, Reverend, 108
Cook, Alfred A., 166
Cook, Clifford B., 166
Cook, Frank R., 166
Couch, Lester, 48
Couhig, Philip H., 64
Cowdery, Arthur E., 164
Creese & Cook, 61, *101*, *119*
Creighton, Ed, 8, 9
Crosby, S. L., 164
Crosby, B. Frank, 164
Crosby, George C., 164
Cross, Roscoe W., 164
Crossman, Ralph T., 166

172

Crowley, Christopher, 127
Crowley, John E., 166
Cullen, Walter, 89
Curtis, George W., 164
Curtis, John, 164
Curtis, Oscar L., 164
Curtis, Robert E., 91, 105
Cyr, Arnold L., 92, *96*, 101, 107, 123, 170
Cyr, Robert J., 92, 111, 115 123, 126, 127, 144, 166
Cyr, Roger L., 13

D
Dale, John W., 164
Dale, William, 164
Danbury, Connecticut, 75
Danforth, Francis E., 164
Danvers Archival Center, 11, 13
Danvers Courier, 25, 27, 33, 41
Danvers Electric Light Department, 48, 63
Danvers Firefighters Relief Association, 150
Danvers Firefighters Union, Local 2038, 116
Danvers Herald, 13, 149
Danvers Historical Society Collections, 41
Danvers Historical Society, 13, 18
Danvers Light Infantry, 36
Danvers Motor Company, 111, 118
Danvers National Bank, 76
Danvers No. 1, 39
Danvers Paper Company, *119*
Danvers Plains Park, 16, 121
Danvers Plains, Mass., 20, 31, 38, 155, 157
Danvers Plaza, 93, 102, 130, 137
Danvers Police Station, *49*
Danvers Rotary Club, 50, 115
Danvers Savings Bank, 97
Danvers State Hospital, 56, 89, 116, 145
Danvers Water Act, 39
Danvers Water Department, 55
Danvers, 17, 154, 155, 156
Danversport Yacht Club, 9, 28
Danversport, Mass., 17, *29*, 31, 32, *38*, 38, 39, 56, 155, 157
Davis, Philip W., 7, 15, 67, 78, 166
DeAngelo, John, 129, 130
DeCoff, George E., 166
DeLuca, David R., 133, 136, 171
Deluge, 45
Dennett, Clarence, 48, 50, 56, 91, 164
Department of Environmental Protection, 144
Derry, New Hampshire, *26*
Devcon Corp., 61
Diaphragm Industries, 97
Dikman, Gilbert, 164
Doane, Melbourne P., 164
Dodge, 58, *59*, 78, 158
Dole & Osgood, 156
Donham & Sweeney, 149
Dougherty, W. W., 164
Dowdell, James L., 164
Dowdell, John H., 164
Dowdell, William, 164
Doyle, Charles H., 15, 66, 67, 69, 70, 72, 85, 91, *96*, 166
Doyle, Daniel J., 46, 164
Doyle, Jeremiah M., 164
Doyle, John E., 164

Doyle, Maurice J., 164
Doyle, W. J., 164
Duffill, Elizabeth, 13
Duffill, John W., Jr., 136, 170
Duke the Dog, 104, 166
Dunnells, Lorenzo, 164
Dunnells, Walter S., 164
Dwinell, Francis W., 15, 61, 67, *74*, 77, 109, 166

E
Eagle, 27, 28, 154
East Greenwich (R.I.) Veteran Firemen's Association, 13, *26*, 157
Eaton, Earl E., 166
Eaton, Irvin S., 164
Eisenhaur, Harold, 166
Elliot, John A., 166
Ellison, David, 135
Ellsworth, John, 71
Ellsworth, Roland W., 166
Emergency One, 111, 116, 118, 150, 158
Emerson, Skip, 8
Ennis, James F., Jr., 166
Erickson, Jim, 9
Erie, 20, 155
Essex County Fire Chiefs's Association, 85, 102
Essex County Foam Bank, 141
Essex Freeman, 31
Essex, Mass., 132, 135, 139

F
Fairlane Condominium, *130*
Falvey, John J., 166
Faneuf, Peter, 150
Farley, John Joseph, Chief, 61, 67, 69, 70, *77*, 78, 83, 84, *87*, 95, *96*, 102, 105, 106, *146*, 166
Farley, John, Sr., 83, 166
Farley, Kevin J., 136, 171
Farley, Michael, 170
Farrell, John J., 166
Farrell, Kevin, 139, 171
Faulkner, Daniel D., 164
Fearer, Myrna, 13
Federal, 17, 154, 155
Ferguson, Charles F., 164
Ferguson, Edward A., *91*, 166
Ferguson, F. T., 164
Ferguson, Ralph W., 89, 166
Ferguson, William H., 164
Ferncroft Business Building, 123
Ferncroft, Mass., 90
Finnegan, P. Francis, 62, *77*, 166
Fire Alarm Dispatch Center, 48
Fire Commissioners, 12
Firehouse Magazine, 115
Firemen's musters, 75
Fireward, 25, 29, 36
First Church, Congregational, *108*
Fitzpatrick, Howard W., 141
Fitzsimmons, Edward F., 164
Flachbart, Robert T., 114, 115, 137, 139, 170
Flynn, Michael J., 164
Flynn, William J., *82*, 166

Folly Hill, 145
Foote, John C., 164
Ford, Arthur M., 166
Ford, Don, 9
Ford, Michael A., 166
Fossa Block, *68*, 71, 123
Foster, Gideon, 21, 155
Foster, Theodore E., 92, *96*, 137, 166
Fox Hill, 23
Franklin Fire Club, 17
Fray, Jack, 9
Friend Box Company, 69
Frost Fish Brook, 33
Fuller, Nathaniel P., 36
Fulton Fire Club, *17*, 18, 41

G
Gaffney, Gerard A., 166
Gallivan, Patrick A., 166
Gamewell Fire Alarm Telegraph, 55, *85*
Gates, Samuel L., 164
Gauthier, Mary J., 166
General Foster, 21, 22, 27, 28, 33, *35*, 154
General Putnam, 20, 28, 31, 32, *34*, *37*, 38, 45, 46, 154, 156
General Scott, 21, 24, 28, 36, 38, 45, 46, 53, *90*, 154, 155, 156, 159
George, James F., 164
Georgetown, Mass., 139
Gilbo, Francis, 166
Giles, Charles S., 164
Gilmor, R. J., Jr., 166
Gilmore, Robert H., *112*, 166
Giroux, Charles T., 166
Gloucester, Mass., 139, *140*, 141, 143
Gnoza, Robert P., 149, 166
Goldthwait, L. W., 164
Goodale, J. Walter, 164
Goodale, Loring B., 164
Goodale, William, 81
Gorup, Frank, 9
Gould, Austin L., 164
Gould, F., 31
Graves, Michael, 171
Graves, William G., 98, 138, 170
Greenwood Fire Apparatus Company, 116
Greenwood, Mass., 117
Griffin, Eben J., 164
Griffin, Frank, 164
Griffin, R. C., 149
Guerrette, Bob, *79*
Guppy, Raymond J., 15, 63, *66*, 67,*74*, 82, 98, 166

H
Hagan, Dana, 123
Haggerty, John F., 166
Halle, Roger, 88
Ham, Herbert C., *44*, 50, *52*, 56, 67, 164
Hamilton, Mass., 113, 135, 139
Hanson, John E., 164
Harbor Master, 144
Hardcover Restaurant, 123
Harrigan, Arthur I., 166
Harrison, Jeffrey J., 102, 170
Hartman, Edwin T., 50, *52*, *54*, 56, 166
Harvey, Barbara, 13

173

Hatch, O., 164
Hathorne, Mass., 89, 90, 93
Haverhill, Mass., 102, 139
Hawkins, Laurice R., 166
Hawks, George A., 164
Hayes, Wilbert K., 166
Heaphy, William, 166
Henry Leather Fire, 115, *117*
Hicks, David W., 166
High Street Headquarters, *148,* 149
Highland Store, 137
Hill, Bryan, 135
Hilton, Clarence, 166
Hilton, Harry L., 164
Hilton, Leaman S., 164
Hobbs, Edwin B., 164
Hobey, Barry, 170
Holbrook Mass., 40, 157
Holten Garden Condominiums, 6
Holten High School, 67
Homan, Harold G., 166
Hook and Ladder, 19, 21, 22, 23, 40, *44,* 156, 157, 164
Hooper, George D., 164
Horgan, James A., 164
Horgan, James M., 69, *82,* 83, 93, *96,* 93, 166
Horgan, John J., 166
Hose reel, *40*
Howard W. Fitzpatrick, 142
Hunneman & Co., 17, 20, 24, *25,* 21, 39, 154, 156
Hunt Memorial Hospital, 7, 105 115, 126, 127, 132, 133, 135, 138, 139
Hunt Nursing Home, 127
Huntley, J. F., 166
Hurd, D. Hamilton, 41
Huse & Co., Samuel, 20, *34,* 41, 154
Hutchinson, Alfred P., 164
Hutchinson, F. P., 165
Hyde, William, Chief, 133, 136

I
Ingraham, Frederick, 126, 135, 171
Ipswich, Mass., 95, 113, 130, 135, 136, 136, 137, 139
Iverson, Howard, 13

J
Jacobs, T. A., 12
Jelison, J. Walter, 165
Johnson, Harry G., 165
Jones Boys, *100*
Jones, Betty, 13
Jones, George E., Jr., 62, 93, 166
Jones, George E., Sr., *47,* 48, 50, *52,* 56, *57,* 67, 109, 159, 165
Jones, Gordon C., 166
Jones, Perley E., 165
Jones, Theodore E., 165
Jordan, Fred S., 166
Joyce, Robert J., Jr., 166
Joyce, Robert J., Sr., *96, 106,* 166

K
Keefe, Jeremiah J., 166
Kelley, Edmund N., 36

Kelley, Joseph E., Jr., 7, 15, 61, 67, 72, 78, 79, 87, 95, *96,* 97, 105, 167
Kelley, Joseph E., Sr., Chief, 6, 50, *51, 52,* 56, *58,* 63, 66, 69, 71, 78, *79,* 83, 84, 85, 167
Kelley, Joseph, Sr., Mrs., 57
Kelley, Thomas, 50
Kelley, W. E., 166
Kelly, Edward H., 165
Kelmar Shoe Co., 50
Kenell, Charles H., 167
Kennedy, Richard D., 127, 135, 170
Kennedy, W. J. C., 33
Keohane, M. H., 13
Kernwood Bridge, 144
Killam, Don, 133
Kimball, Frank W., 165
Kimball, George, 129
Kimball, Warren, 12
King, Edward, Governor, 8
King, Melvin E., 69, 167
Kinsella, Joseph M., 67, 72, *74,* 167
Kirwan, Thomas, 41
Knox Automobile Company, 48
Kobierski, Kenneth, 171
Kontos, Thomas, 71
Kowalski, Dorothy, 126
Kuell, Alfred H., 167, *96*
Kuell, Charles H., 71, *77, 96,* 167

L
La Fortune, Arthur P., 167
LaChance, Arthur T., 167
LaChance, George N., *82, 96,* 167
LaChance, Joseph, 167
Lachance, Ernest J., 165
Landolphi, Francis M., 89
LaPointe, Paul, 171
LaPointe, Robert A., 98, 170
LaPointe, Ronald, 167
Lawrence, A. C., Leather Company, 48
Lawrence, Barbara, 13
Lawton, Bert, 167
Layman, Lloyd, 67
Lear, James J., 167
Learoyd, J. A., 32
Lennon, Francis, 133
Lesley, Edward S., 21, 22, 24, 41, 154
Leverick, Edward B., 40, 156
Lewis, Jerry, 116
Lexington Battle Monument, *35*
Liberty Tree Mall, 99
Lindell, A., 165
Linehan, David J., 167
Little, George, 165
Littlefield, Austin L., 165
Littlewood, Pete, 88
Logan Airport, 102, 113, 141
Lonergan, James, 141
Lord & Herlihy, 64
Lord, Arthur R., 167
Lowell, 106
Loyal Order of Moose, 78
Lynch, John P., 165
Lynch, John, 66, 67, 78, 167
Lynn, Mass., 95, 106, 110, 113, 111, 113, 131, 133, 136, 137, 139

Lyons Ambulance Service, 126, 132, 133, 138, 139
Lyons, Bernard, *74, 82,* 86, 167
Lyons, Jerimiah P., 167
Lyons, John, 88
Lyons, William C., 138, 165

M
MacDonald, James, *44,* 165
MacLean, Valentine, 167
Madden, Mrs., 103
Madison, James V., 167
Madison, John D., 56, 63, 69, 72, 86, 167, *169*
Mains, James H., 165
Maitlant Brothers, 141
Major Chase, 45, *153*
Malden, Mass., 135, 136, 137, 139
Manchester-by-the Sea, Mass., 95, 131, 133, 136, 139
Manning, Donald P., 167
Manning, John, 165
Maple, Fred J., 167
Maple, Thomas E., 167
Maple Street Congregational Church, 9, 10, 30, 32, *60,* 61, *62, 169*
Marblehead, Mass., 113, 132, 133, 137, 139
Marquis, Wayne, 111, 114, 149
Marshall's Harness Shop, *94,* 97
Marshall, Edwin S., 95
Martin, Leland E., Jr., Chief, 6, 11, 15, 69, *73, 74, 76, 79, 96,* 101, *106, 114, 119, 140, 146,* 149, 167
Martin, Christopher, 167
Martin, Connie, 13, 142
Martin, Walter, 167
Martin, William W., 165
Masonic Temple, 48
Massachusetts Firefighters Academy, 13, 149
Massachusetts General Court, 18
Matthew Hooper, 40, 45
Maurais, Charles, 13, 132, 133
Maxim, 116
Maynard, Francis O., 91, 97, 167
Maynard, Leo F., 167
McCarthy, David F., 165
McCarthy, John F., 165
McDonald, Howard, 88
McDonald, W. M., 165
McFadden, Daniel J., 84
McFarland, Fred, 167
McInnis, Charles E., Jr., 167
McInnis, James A., 79, 92, 136, 167
McKay, Barry, Chief, 133, 141, 142
McKeigue, Frank, 165
McKinnon, Charles H., 165
McLaughlin, Edward F., 13, 167, 171
McNamara, Ann, 11, 13
McPherson, James, 115, 123, 133, 135, 171
McTernen, Charles, 46, 95
Meadows, 69
Medomak, 21
Memorial Day Parade, *96,* 108
Mercier, J. A., 95
Metcalf, Lester, 98
Michalski, Henry, Jr., 129
Michelson's Candy Store, 97

Middleton, Mass., 63, 93, 95, 102, 113, 127, 129, 131, 132, 138, 139
Mill Pond, 6, 57
Miller, John T., 165
Mills, Gerald R., 102, 136, 139, 171
Minnehan, Jermiah, 92
Moby Dick, *100*, 101, 103 159, *162*
Modest, Walter B., 167
Mogavero, Antonio, 56
Monty, F., 167
Moreland, Ronald L., 127, 136, 167
Moriarty, Daniel D., 165
Moriarty, John J., 165
Morin, David, 133, 170
Morin, Sylvio J., *82*, 167
Morrell, William A., 165
Morris, Eugene I., 13
Morrison, Herbert E., *44*, 165
Morrissey, John, 167
Morse, George M., 165
Moser, Joseph W., 165
Mugridge, Parker P., 167
Mugridge, Wallace M., 167
Mullaly, Charles D., 167
Mullaly, Harold T., 167
Murphy Company, E. J., 117
Murphy, J. J., 165
Murphy, William F., 69, 101, 167

N
Nahant, Mass., 110
Nash, George, 144
Neal, Timothy A., 165
Neal, William F., 165
Neary, Matthew F., 167
Nesson Block, 105, 111
New England Fire & History Museum, 13, *37*, 157
New England Fire Chiefs' Association, 63, 118
New England Fire Insurance Rating Association, 55, 88
New Mills, Mass., 17, 20, 21, 22, 25, 28, 139, 142, 155
Niagara, 17, 28, 154
Nightingale, J. Ellis, 165
Nimblett, B. T., 167
Nimblett, Charles J., 63, 167
Nimblett, Frank D., 165
Nimblett, Leo D., 63, 67, 165, 167
Nimblett, William F., 165
Noonan, Edward J., *85*
Noonan, John M., 67, 69, *74*, 85, 93, 109, 167
North Andover, Mass., 132, 139
North Danvers, Mass., 32, 34
North Parish, 20, 21, 37
North Reading, Mass., 113, 130, 132, 136, 139
North Shore Ambulance, 139
North Shore Community College, 8, 12, 98, 106, 110, 111, 149
Noyes Shoe Factory, 34

O
O'Breen, Daniel, 31
O'Brian, John H., 165
O'Connell, Timothy, 129
O'Connor, Thomas J., 13
O'Keefe, Jeremiah, 165

O'Keefe, Joe, 8, 106
O'Malley, Joseph, 133
Oby, Maurice C., 28
Ocean, 21, *22*, 28, *29*, 31, 32, 33, 35, *38*, 38, 39, *39*, 45, 46, 53, 76, 154, 156
Olmstead, L. W., 165
Orpheum Theatre, 97
Osborn, A. C., 36
Osgood, Richard K., 115, 133, 167
Osgood, Robert G., 13, 79, 85, 92, *101*, 167
Oulton, Richard L., 13

P
Page, John, 31
Palmer, Dean, Chief, 8, 85, 102, 110
Park Lane Condominiums, 131, 133, 135, 136, *137*
Parker Grain Co., George H., 99, *100*
Parker's Gristmill, 95
Parker's Island, 142, *143*
Parsons, Robert, 170
Passaconaway, 76
Peabody Institute Library, *47*, 57
Peabody Story, 41
Peabody, George, 34, *35*
Peabody, Mass., *25*, *26*, 56, 61, 63, 93, 113, 115, 129, 130, 131, 133, 135, 139, 155, 156
Peabody, Ralph P., 165
Pearson, William B., *52*, 167, *169*
Pease Air Force Base, 102
Pedrick Woods, 78
Pelletier, Donald F., 89
Pelonzi, Kenneth, Chief, 129, 130, 136
Pennell, Everett E., 167
Pennell, Lloyd E., *74*, 167
Pennell, Warren, *44*, 165
Pennell, Wilson H., 167
Perley, Osborn, 165
Perry, Charles H., 165
Perry, Chris, 13
Perry, Christine M., 171
Perry, Michael E., 136, 150, 170
Perry, Sarafine F., 79, 167
Pete's Garage, 69
Petronzio, Albert F., 102, 171
Pettipas, John B., 102, 167
Phinney, Byron, 165
Phinney, James H., 167
Piccolo, Steve, 111
Pierce Arrow, *57*, 158
Pierce, Stephen, 167
Pike & Whipple, 156
Pinkham, Harry, 13
Pirsch, *59*, 64, 65, *70*, 87, *100*, 117, 150, 158
Pirsch, Peter, 57, 98
Pitman, H. W., 165
Pitman, Jacob B., *44*, 165
Pitman, Ralph E., 56, 167
Pollard, Charles A., Jr., 88, 167
Porter, Walter E., 165
Powers, John J., 165
Prendergast, Stephen L., 150, 171
Price, David E., 123, 127, 167
Price, Edward R., 165
Putnam Lodge, 83, 87, *88*
Putnam, Archelaus, 99

Putnam, Burton L., 165
Putnam, Calvin, Lumber Company, 72
Putnam, Edward E., 165
Putnam, Israel, General, 32, 155
Putnam, John, 99
Pyburn, Richard T., 91, 171
Pyburn, Robert J., Sr., 167
Pyburn, Robert, 136, 170

Q
Quinn, John, 8, 110
Quint, 150, *151*, 159

R
Rackliff, Walter F., 165
Ransom, Harold A., 167
Rat Hole, 71
Red Cross, 59
Reedy, Joan, 11
Reformer, 20, 155
Regan, Francis Daniel, 53, 56, 69, *73*, 167
Reid, Peter, 165
Reid, William, 165
Revere, Mass., 139
Richards, Daniel, 33
Richards, George, 33
Richardson, Ernest S., 95
Richers, Eddie, 13
Rigby, George J., 165
Rigby, William E., 167
Riggs, John, Jr., 167
Robinson, Henry P., 167
Rock, Percy, 167
Rockport, Mass., 136, 139
Romano, Paul, 133
Rosewood IV, 111
Rough and Ready, 39, 157
Rowe, Frederick, 167
Rumsey Manufacturing Co., 156
Rundlett, George O., 165
Russell, Austin S., 165
Russell, Edmund N., 165
Russell, Percy E., 165
Russell, Vernon C., 167
Russell, Walter J., 165
Ryan & Co., James T., 156
Ryan, Joseph R., 167
Ryan, Michael J., 165
Ryan, William B., 167
Ryback, Richard, Rear Admiral, 141

S
Sacco, Frank, 170
Sail Carriage, 19, 21, 22, 23
Salem Evening News, 12, 13, 109
Salem Hospital, 136, 113, 131, *132*, 135, 137, 139
Salem Observer, 31, 41
Salem, Mass., 30, 33, 34, 48, 63, 93, 95, 144
Sandy Beach, 144
Sanford Airfield, 78
Sanford, George B., 97
Sanford, Maine, 110
Santorella, Anthony D., 91, 167
Santorella, Joseph, 79, 107, 167
Sargent, George A., 167
Saugus, Mass., 130, 136, 139

Scanlon, Joe, 110
Scanlon, Kirk R., 167
School Street Station, 46, *49*
Scollins, Jim, 106
Seabrook, New Hampshire, 76
Senate, 97
Serratore, Nicholas, 136, 171
Seventeenth Massachusetts Regiment, 36
Shackley, Clarence, *47*, 165
Shattuck, David S., *30*
Shea, John F., 165
Shea, Patrick J., 165
Sheppard, Eli, 167
Shively, Harold, 106
Siesta Sleep Shop, 111
Silva, Olivia, 137, 138
Silvester, Joshua, 32
Simpson, Charles E., 167
Simpson, Charles J., 167
Skinner, Harold, 167
Skinner, Hollis G., 56, 98, 167, *169*
Skinner, Michael C., 98, 107, 111, 115, *121*, 126, 131, 133, 135, 136, 139, *140*, 141, 142, 144, 167
Skinner, Ronald B., 98, 114, 115, 126, 127, 170
Skinner, Walton F., 15, *97*, 98, 167
Sleeper, Albert C., 165
Small, Frank J., 167
Small, James H., 167
Smith, Earl W., 167
Smith, Ford R., 133, 171
Smith, Frederick, 165
Smith, Matthew, 170
Smith, P. G., 167
Smith, "Rusty", 102
Smith, W. W., 36
Smith, Wayne G., 167
Smorczewski, Marc, 170
Snow, George H., 102, 126, 171
Sousa, Joseph R., 13
South Congregational Church, 30, 32, 41
South Danvers, Mass., 17, *35*, 37, 38, 156
South Parish, 17, 20, 21, 24, *25*, 32, 37, 155, 157
Spaulding Building, *51*
Spaulding, Samuel W., 48
Spears, Edward J., 165
Spears, Thomas F., 167
Spink David, 13
Spite Bridge, 72
Spofford, Robert, 13
Sprague, E. Walter, Jr., 167
Sprout, John, 165
St. John's Prep, 79
Staples, Charles H., 165
Staples, George E., 165
Steam engine, 38, 39, 40
Stearns, Carlton M., 63
Steele, Leslie J., 165
Steutermann, John H., 165
Stevens, Phillip, 135
Studley, George, 165
Sturtevant, R. F., 7, 15, 67, 78, *91*, 93, 167
Sullivan's Garage, 72
Sullivan, David C., 107, 167
Sullivan, David J., 165

Sullivan, David, 115, 133, 135, 136, 137, 141, 170
Sullivan, DeWayne, 171
Sullivan, James F., 167
Sullivan, John F., 165
Sullivan, Mo, 137, 138
Sullivan, P. J., 165
Sullivan, Raymond A., 167
Sullivan, Richard J., 92, 107, 171
Sullivan, Timothy J., 165
Supreme Roast Beef Shop, 111
Sutton, William, General, 22, 24, 155, 157
Swampscott, Mass., 95, 131, 133, 133, 136, 136, 139
Sweet, Newton, 149
Sweetser, Frank E., 165
Swindell, Elden A., 46, *90*, 165
Swindell, Frederick W., 167
Szypko Bridge, 99

T
Talbot, Francis H., *82*, 167
Talbot, Henry J., *82*, *96*, 167
Tapley's Village, 21, 22, 24, 34
Tapley, Harriet Silvester, *Chronicles of Danvers*, 41
Tapleyville, Mass., 21, 38, 48, *54*, 90, 155
Taylor, Mollie, 13
Thayer, Ephraim & Stephen, 17, 154
The Great Big Fire Engine Book, 15
Thibodeau, Adolphus, 165
Thomas, Henry H., 167
Tibbetts, Charles A., *44*, 165
Tibbetts, Willard P., 165
Tibbetts, William F., 165
Tobin Bridge, 106
Toomey, Francis, 170
Topping, Ann, 133
Topsfield, Mass., 58, 63, 75, 113, 127, 131, 139, 159
Torrent, 20, *21*, 24, *25*, 27, 28, 154
Towle, David, 117, 118
Town Meeting, 18, 23, 39, 41, 46, 48, 64, 66, 69, 149
Townsend, Harry S., 165
Traicoff, George, 111
Trask, Charles, 78
Trask, Gardner S., Sr., *14*, 15, 61, 63, *67*, *76*, 167
Trask, Gardner, Jr., 15
Trask, Mildred D., 13
Trask, Percy C., 165
Trask, Richard B., 11, 12, 15, *40*, 50, 108
Travers, William, 13
Trefrey, William, 126, 144, 171
Tufts, Aaron P., *47*, 165
Tufts, Arthur S., 167
Tufts, Lester B., 165
Tufts, Sherman A., 165
Tutko, Henry T., 171
Tutko, James P., 102, 136, 143, 144, *146*, 149, 170
Tweed, William, 20
Twilight League, 61, 84
Twiss, Frank, 129

U
Universalist Church, 34

V
Vaillancourt, Fred, 79
Vaillancourt, Wilfred A., 13, *74*, *86*, 167
Ventron Corporation, 113, 114, 118, 119
ViCliff's Restaurant, 85, *86*
Village Bank, 32
Volunteer, 24, *26*, 27, 28, 154, 156

W
Wadsworth Cemetery, 10
Waldoborough Historical Society, 13, 21, 155
Walker, Charles H., 165
Walker, Watson J., 165
Walker, William H., 165
Wallace, Hardy P., 89, 167
Ward LaFrance, *100*, 100, 103, 158
Waterlac Company, *162*
Waters River, 61
Weaver, William J., 167
Webb, Ernest S., 165
Weeks, Alan, 102, 171
Weeks, Arnold N., Jr., 102, 108, 117, 170
Weld, William, Governor, 8
Wells Drug Store, *70*, 71
Wells, John A., 41
Wenham, Mass., 113, 127, 131, 133, 135, 136, 139
Wessell, Richard C., 10, 13, 61, 91, 92, 106, 109, 113, 115, *121*, 127, 129, 131, 133, 135, 136, 137, 144, 150, 170
Wessell, Jay, 136, 171
West Peabody, Mass., 17
Westfield, Mass., 157
Wetzel, Marjorie, 13
Weymouth, Mass., 157
Whalen, James E., 167
White, Harvey E., *44*, 165
White, Joseph E., 167
Whitman, Carl N., 165
Whittier, Joseph, 46
Wilkins, Frank A., 167
Williams School, 72
Williams, Chester, 165
Williams, George E., 165
Williams, Myron A., 167
Williamson, Kirk R., 13
Wilson, George A., 48, *74*, 167
Wolkin, Ed, 13
Wood Co., Phillip A., 75
Wood, Phillip A., 58
Woodman, Frank B., 165
Woods, P. J., 159
Woodvale, 86, *107*
Woolley, Bill, 13
World War II, 58, *59*
Wormstead, Mary Jane, 13
Wrest, George, 165
Wright, Willy, 88

Y
Yates, James, *44*, 165
York Steak House, 103
Your Market, *92*, 93

Z
Zeus, 141, 142
Zollo's Barber Shop, 72
Zollo, Paul G., 12
Zollo, Richard P., 41